blue
rider
press

THE
NEW OLD
ME

THE
NEW OLD
ME

— My Late-Life Reinvention —

MEREDITH MARAN

BLUE RIDER PRESS | NEW YORK

blue
rider
press

An imprint of Penguin Random House LLC
375 Hudson Street
New York, New York 10014

Copyright © 2017 by Meredith Maran
Penguin supports copyright. Copyright fuels creativity, encourages diverse voices,
promotes free speech, and creates a vibrant culture. Thank you for buying an authorized
edition of this book and for complying with copyright laws by not reproducing, scanning,
or distributing any part of it in any form without permission. You are supporting
writers and allowing Penguin to continue to publish books for every reader.

Blue Rider Press is a registered trademark and its colophon is a trademark of
Penguin Random House LLC

ISBN 9780399574139

Printed in the United States of America
1   3   5   7   9   10   8   6   4   2

Book design by Gretchen Achilles

*Penguin is committed to publishing works of quality and integrity.
In that spirit, we are proud to offer this book to our readers; however,
the story, the experiences, and the words are the author's alone.*

In memory of Sidney Melvin Maran

July 18, 1927–April 4, 2013

Sometimes I think it would be easier to avoid old age,
to die young, but then you'd never complete your life,
would you? You'd never wholly know you.

—MARILYN MONROE

The New Old Me begins with my move to Los Angeles and focuses on the three years that followed, not on what happened before. To protect other people's privacy and the integrity of the storytelling, I've compressed time frames, refrained from writing about my children, and altered identifying details and names.

PART ONE

EMPTY

PROLOGUE

When the knife slips, I feel nothing. Everything freezes: the knife, my breath, time. I go numb. Dumb.

I know that I've cut my finger, and I know that it's bad. But it's too soon for pain. I hold the ring finger of my right hand to my face and I see things I shouldn't: blood, tendon. Is that bone?

I grab a dish towel with my good hand and wrap it around my bleeding hand and thrust the mess into the air.

Instinctively I call out my wife's name. For fifteen years, that's what I did whenever something terrible or wonderful happened. I called out my wife's name. My wife is four hundred miles away, but old habits die hard. *Nearest emergency room,* I tell myself. *Hurry.*

I don't know where the nearest hospital is, or how to get there. This is Los Angeles, not Manhattan, my childhood hometown of the geometric grid; not Oakland, where I lived for the past thirty years, with its numbered east-west avenues. I don't know where anything is, nor how to get there in L.A.'s twisted gridlock of four-lane streets and scrimmaging intersections.

The nearest hospital, Siri tells me, is fifteen minutes away. "Everything in L.A. is fifteen minutes away," the locals say, "and it takes an hour to get there." The dish towel on my finger is soaked with blood already. I hope this time the locals are wrong.

I replace the towel with a fresh one, grab my purse and my keys, maneuver my upraised arm and then the rest of me into the driver's seat of my car. I don't want to be in the driver's seat of my car. I want to be in the passenger seat of my wife's car.

I drive south on Silver Lake Boulevard, straight into the setting sun. At the intersection of Silver Lake and Sunset, Siri tells me to turn north. If I knew where north was, I wouldn't be talking to Siri. It's easier to turn left than right without the use of my right hand. I decide that "north" is "left."

I pass the sprawling Scientology campus on Sunset and pull into the ER's circular drive. A sign on the wall reads DROP-OFFS ONLY. NO PARKING.

L.A. hiking trails have valets. Real estate open houses. Ice-cream parlors. Boutiques. But not the ER, where a valet is actually needed. Not here, where the not-rich people go.

I decide against arguing with the security guard that I'm both driver and patient, and therefore entitled to leave my car here while I drop myself off. I drive to the nearest garage, spin up and up and up the circular ramp, find a space on the fourth floor. I'm too dizzy to search for the elevator. I get dizzier, trudging down the urine-soaked stairwell, right hand held high.

The ER doors slide open. I follow the receptionist's eyes to my right hand. Apparently the newspaper rule "If it bleeds, it leads" also applies here. She jumps up, rushes me into a treatment room, and runs out. A tall, balding doctor appears, snapping on gloves, and then a nurse, her hands already gloved. Neither of them makes eye contact with me. Neither of them says a word. The nurse lowers my hand from above my head, removes the dish towel, and deposits it in the hazardous waste bin. She lines the doctor's lap with blue-and-white Chux and sets my right hand into his upturned palm. His hand and the Chux turn red.

The doctor squints at my wedding ring. "We'll need to cut that off," he says.

"You can't do that," I say.

The doctor raises his eyebrows at me. I'm sure he sees plenty of crazies in this ER; how would he know I'm not one of them? Maybe I should tell him about the Dr. Phil moment I had yesterday, when I actually thought, It's time to move on with my life, and I looked at my wedding ring, wondering what it would feel like to take it off for the first time in a decade, to be me without it, without the story it used to tell, and then closed my eyes and pulled it off.

I put the ring in my underwear drawer and closed the drawer. I looked at my left hand without my ring on it and put the ring back on. I unhooked the gold chain around my neck and hung the ring on the chain and looked at my left hand without my ring on it and took the ring off the chain and put it back on my finger.

Problem identified. What I want is not to move on with my life. What I want is my old life back.

How long, I wondered, will it take me to stop wanting that? Will I be seventy, eighty, ninety, single and still wearing this wedding ring?

Baby steps, I told myself, and put the ring on my right hand instead of my left. It felt weird—scary, sad—but also accurate: not exactly married, not exactly not.

"I can't let you cut that ring off," I tell the doctor.

He frowns. The nurse whisks the bloody Chux off his lap and replaces them with a clean set.

"I'm sure you cut wedding rings off all the time," I say. "But my wife and I are separated. I'm still hoping—"

The doctor stares at me. There is a certain narrowing of his eyes, a certain clenching of his jaw. I realize that although it's 2012 and gay marriage is legal in seven states and we're in one of the world's gayest cities, this white-haired, white-faced man is not happy to be holding the hand of a woman who has a wife.

I watch as his conscience kicks in, or the diversity training the hospital made him take, or the nondiscrimination policies they require him to uphold. He reassembles his face. Too late. Message received.

I've been gay in America long enough to know Rule One: Physical Safety Above All. I don't want this guy to get sloppy on the job because he's sewing up a smartass, half-married, geriatric lesbian who doesn't even know which hand a wedding ring belongs on.

I don't want to share any more of my innards with this doctor than the parts of me he's already holding. I won't tell him that until I got into my car and drove to Los Angeles three months ago, I thought I knew how the final phase of my life would go, and it didn't involve Los Angeles, let alone a solo trip to the Sunset Boulevard ER. I thought the choices I'd made had set me up for a sweet ride the rest of the way.

Despite my boomer-appropriate countercultural predilections, I'd turned out to be a fair to middling grown-up. I'd surrounded myself with smart, loving people; saved money when I could and spent it frugally when I couldn't; worked hard at a career I loved and was good at; renovated a three-story Victorian on the Oakland/Berkeley border and lived there, while its value tripled, for twenty-three years.

Most auspiciously, I was ecstatically married. And I was sure I always would be.

"Let me try to get it off myself," I tell the doctor.

He holds up my bleeding hand in the narrow space between our faces. "You've cut yourself to the bone. If infection sets in, you could lose your finger. You could even go septic. Do you know what that means?"

"Please," I say. "Let me try."

"I'll give you fifteen minutes. Nurse Santos will help you." The doctor beckons to the nurse and they both leave the room.

Nurse Santos returns with an armful of supplies. She sets a plastic bucket of ice, a giant tube of K-Y Jelly, and a pile of Chux on the tray in front of me. She plunges my finger into the bucket of ice, waits a few beats, pulls my finger out, slathers it with K-Y Jelly, and hands it back to me.

I close my eyes and I pull and twist and pull and twist. The ring is stuck. It's a vise grip tightening on my finger. It hurts like hell.

The doctor reappears. "It's time," he says. "So. Which would you rather keep? Your finger or your wedding ring?"

As he speaks, Nurse Santos gathers up what remains of our efforts and assembles a workstation on the rolling table: a neat row of syringes, scissors, thread, and some unrecognizable scary-looking instruments sealed in blue plastic bags.

The doctor reaches for my hand. I grab it back.

"Any jeweler will be able to fix that ring," the nurse says.

The doctor rolls his shiny metal stool closer to me and grabs my right hand and shoves something cold and hard between my ring finger and my ring. I feel a sharp click. The nurse takes my hand before I can look at it. She sets a small plastic specimen jar next to me. The doctor's face floats near mine. He positions a syringe over my hand.

"This will numb you," he says. "Then we'll sew you up."

I turn away so I can't see what he's about to do. Instead my eyes turn to the specimen jar. In it, the broken circle of my wedding ring.

ONE

MAY 20, 2012

stand in the living room of the house I've lived in for the past twenty-three years, trying to imagine what I'll need for the life that comes next.

I raised two sons in this house, wrote nine books, threw dozens of parties, earned and spent and lost money, celebrated birthdays from thirty-eight to sixty. For the last fifteen years I lived here with the love of my life.

What to take? Clothes. No matter where I end up living or what I end up doing, I'll need clothes. I climb the stairs to the attic, start grabbing armloads of hangers, trudging up- and downstairs until my car is full.

I move through the other rooms quickly, numbly, grabbing small things as I go. Curl gel. Milk frother. Zoloft, Ambien, Ativan. Potato scrubber. Framed photographs of my kids, my friend Patricia, my wife and me.

Many times in the past three years, I've tried on the idea of leaving. Each time I recoiled from the thought. Now that I'm doing it, I'm not one inch closer to wanting to go. I'm standing beside my packed car, nailed to the moment. There must be a way to save this marriage, I think for maybe the five millionth time.

"Meredith?" My seventy-seven-year-old neighbor, Vonna, is taking her daily constitutional from her end of the block to ours. She peers into my car.

"You ladies going on vacation?" she asks.

"Just me," I answer. For better and for worse, I've always told pretty much everyone pretty much everything. Now only my wife, my family, and my closest friends know that I'm moving to L.A. I barely believe it myself.

I hug Vonna good-bye.

"Hurry back, you hear?" she says.

Not gonna happen, I think. "Will do," I say, and I get in my car and go.

DRIVING SOUTH through the barren moonscape that flanks Interstate 5, I flip through stations on my car radio, attempting to muffle my thoughts. Spanish-language stations, Jesus stations, bubblegum-pop stations, static. The narrative in my head, though, is perfectly clear.

"My marriage is over." I say it out loud.

"Why?" is the question. The answer is "I don't know."

My wife and I were the happiest couple anyone, including us, had ever known. I attributed most of our glory to her. In past relationships I was a lover and a fighter. My wife was the keeper of our peace; she valued harmony above all things. She lived in a meadow, we always said; I lived in a cave. Why would I lure her into my darkness when she beckoned me toward wildflowers and light?

Conflict between us was rare. When it happened, she simply stopped talking to me for an hour or a day. Then she'd crawl into bed beside me. "Let's make up," she'd purr. Gratefully I'd take her into my arms.

As the years went by, we bragged about it: Two fights in five years. Three fights in ten.

The harmony felt so good, I never considered its consequences. I went on believing the story of us, the one we told and retold. I was perfect for her and she was perfect for me and we were perfectly happy in our perfect, friction-free marriage. Turns out things that needed to be said were not said. Turns out the price of harmony-at-all-costs was high.

Overnight, our beauty went ugly. No fighting one day; nothing but fighting the next. We tried marriage counseling. Individual therapy. Trial separations. There were tearful, transitory reconciliations, wrenching angry letters left where love notes used to be—packed into each other's suitcases, slipped into the books we were reading, into each other's lingerie drawers. For three years we wrestled, trying to find our way back to each other, ourselves, the once-magical us. Nothing worked.

My self-confidence, never my strong suit, was flagging. My career was circling the drain. Interspersed with brief intervals of employment, I'd managed to eke out a living as a freelance writer for forty-five years. But then 9/11 and the 2008 crash happened, and the magazine and book publishing businesses tanked, turning my income into a shadow of its former self. Despite my penchant for taking things personally, I knew that the problem wasn't mine alone. Writer friends were taking teaching jobs, if they could get them, moving to cheaper cities, marrying for health insurance and rent. None of those stopgaps was an option for me.

Throughout 2011 and 2012, the cascade of catastrophes continued. On the first day of our third trial separation, I got an e-mail from my socially responsible investment advisor, copying my wife, informing us that she'd made an accounting error. The $80,000 she'd reported as the balance in my account actually belonged in my wife's. My balance was an even zero. Days of frantic forensic accounting failed to make my savings reappear.

So when a miracle appeared in my inbox in the form of a copywriting job offer in Los Angeles, I didn't hesitate. A job four hundred miles away wouldn't replace my savings or restore the joy I'd had and lost with my wife. But I needed money, and my wife and I needed a break. In a rare moment of unanimity, she and I agreed that I should take the job. I was sorrow-struck, not crazy. I walked through that one open door.

I canceled my therapy appointments and my hiking dates and had my mail forwarded to my new office and arranged to crash with a Bay Area expat friend and her new Angeleno man and said good-bye to my friends and family.

The farewell I'd dreaded most had been averted in the saddest possible way. Last night I'd gone to bed believing that *something* would happen between us before I left this morning. My wife would creep into the guest-room bed with me during the night, or bring me tea in the morning, or call to me from our marriage bed.

But no. I'd awakened early this morning to walls that rang

with emptiness. When I went downstairs to check the driveway, I'd found that her car was gone.

DRIVING, DRIVING. My phone rings. My wife, I think.

"Where are you?" asks my best friend, Celia. It was Celia's house I ran to, the first time the fighting got bad enough for me to leave. The reason for my arrival on her doorstep was almost as hard on Celia as it was on me. She used to call my wife and me "Mom and Mom" because being with us, she said, made her feel like a happy, secure child.

"On Highway Five. Passing that disgusting cattle ranch."

"So you did it," Celia says.

"I'm doing it," I say.

THREE HOURS LATER my phone rings again. My wife?

"Where are you?" asks my friend Emily.

"In a smelly rest-stop bathroom. About halfway there."

"So you did it," Emily says.

"I'm doing it," I say.

SIRI GUIDES ME OFF the freeway and into the steep switchback streets of Laurel Canyon. I wind through twisty, narrow streets beaded with pink and purple bougainvillea and towering, fuzzy phallic cacti, under a sky so blue and a sun so yellow they look like a first-grader's rendering of sky and sun.

I feel like I'm in another country, not the southern half of the same state. The houses and gardens and stone paths I drive by are labyrinthine, lush, boho mysterious, yet oddly familiar. Maybe I'm having memories of *Laurel Canyon*, one of my all-time-favorite movies. Or maybe my kind of people, with my kind of funky style, live here.

I've been so focused on what I'm losing, moving to Los Angeles, that I haven't considered what, besides a paycheck, I might gain. I realize now that I'm not just leaving someplace familiar. I'm also landing someplace new. The place that turned fairy tales into talkies and orange groves into the film factory for the world. The place where Norma Jean became Marilyn Monroe.

Driving more slowly now, I turn left onto Lookout Mountain Avenue. "Your destination is on the right," Siri says. I stop in front of a fairy-tale cottage draped in lime-green grapevines, its arched door peeling teal paint, its front garden a jungle of overgrown lemon trees and sky-high agave spires and artichoke plants gone mad. I imagine Joni Mitchell, lady of this canyon, living here with Graham Nash; Crosby and Stills dropping by to jam.

I maneuver my car into a parking space the shape of a fusilli, unfold my stiff, fusilli-shaped body, and step out into blinding sunlight. Like Marilyn Monroe and Joni Mitchell and legions of desperate dreamers before me, I've arrived.

TWO

Jules answers my knock with a distracted hug and a tinfoil-covered cardboard box under his arm. His face is kind and gentle and unmoved by the sight of me, and no wonder. We barely know each other. Clara's the one who offered me their couch. And Clara's away for a month, visiting friends back east. "Jules gets lonely when I'm gone," she'd said when I called to beg the favor. "He'll be happy to have your company."

"That'll make one of us," I'd said, and Clara had sighed, with empathy or with compassion fatigue.

Until this moment, I haven't considered the reality of my new lifestyle. I'd be sharing a house with a guy I barely know. I've done that before, but never without sex involved.

"Oh. Hello. You're just in time." Jules steps out of his house, closing the door behind him.

"Hello," I say. "In time for what?"

"We'll unload your car when we get back," he says. "Follow me."

I'm a hiker, but I have trouble keeping Jules's pace. "Thanks for letting me stay with you," I say.

"Of course, of course," Jules says without inflection. It occurs to me that Clara might have overstated his willingness to have me around.

Trotting to Jules's walk, I wonder if every hike I take for the rest of my life will remind me of my favorite-ever hiking buddy, Patricia. She and I were the same age, both writers, moms, wives, and underbudgeted fashionistas. We had our differences, too. I didn't quite graduate high school. Patricia was a Chinese scholar, fluent in Mandarin and Cantonese. Brilliant, bitingly witty, and beautiful, she was chemo-bald the day we met at a writer's retreat, shocked to find each other wearing the same fleece jacket from the same obscure French line. Mine was black; Patricia's was a rich shade of olive green.

"I almost bought it in that color," I said. "It's beautiful."

"The black is easier to wear," she said. "You made a good call."

Over dinner that night Patricia told me calmly that she was several years past the life expectancy for her metastasized breast cancer. But her fourteen-year-old daughter, Maya, needed her, and so did her husband, Mark, and she had a book to finish. As long as she could, Patricia said, she was simply going to refuse to die.

For the next few years, once or twice a week, Patricia and her Irish setter, Blue, and I would meet at the trailhead, often exchanging some item of clothing that one thought the other would like. After our brief parking-lot fashion show, we'd huff and puff up and down the redwood mountains together, Blue gamboling, Patricia and I dissecting the high-stakes struggles we shared: troubled childhoods, troubled marriages, troubled kids, troubled manuscripts.

When my wife and I were at the start of our free fall, my wife joked to Patricia that if she ever broke a hiking date with me, our marriage would be over by the end of the day. It wasn't really a joke. My wife knew that Patricia spent hours explaining and defending my wife to me, because Patricia loved my wife, and she loved the way our marriage had been before it went bad, and, I realized later, Patricia probably knew she was dying and she didn't want me to be alone when she did. Week after week, mile after mile, Patricia counseled me to be patient, to hear the love as well as the anger in the things my wife said to me, to find compassion in myself even when my wife couldn't find it in herself or in me.

The day after our hike one Tuesday in November 2011, Patricia landed in the hospital. "Your friend has the strongest will I've ever seen," her nurse told me when I took her aside to ask about Patricia's prognosis. "But at some point, the body wins." Two months later, Patricia came home to die.

I left Patricia's deathbed and I got into bed in our guest room and I didn't get up for a week. During that week my wife never came into my room to comfort me, and I never sought her comfort, and after that it was no longer possible to deny or ignore how broken our marriage was. Looking back at it now, I see that the start of my life without Patricia was also the start of my single life.

At Patricia's memorial, a musician friend played her favorite song, Leonard Cohen's "Hallelujah," and in his voice I heard Patricia's, her rare blend of brilliance and tenderness and rage, and

I doubled over in my chair, sobbing. My wife put her hand on my back and the gesture felt jarring to me, a habit or a public performance or a last shot of her love, a purge that would free her to rid herself of me.

After Patricia died I tried hiking alone. I tried hiking our trails with our mutual friends, wonderful writer-women who missed her, too. Conversations with these not-Patricias made my ears ache for the special language she and I spoke together, the soothing sound of her voice.

In case I thought it couldn't get any worse, here I am in a strange place on some strange mission, hiking with a stranger.

"Where are we going?" I ask Jules.

"You don't know what's happening tonight?"

I shake my head.

"Tonight we'll see an annular eclipse from Earth for the first time in twenty years." Jules stops walking and pulls a phone out of his crumpled cargo shorts. He taps a few keys and shows me a photograph of a black moon encircled by a gold band of sun.

"This was the last annular eclipse," he says. "Makes the sun look like a wedding ring, doesn't it."

I follow Jules onto a rocky outcropping that juts over the canyon. Along its edge, people are gathered in clumps, parents holding kids' hands, couples with their arms around each other, groups of people in lawn chairs with beers in their cup holders. Many of them are peering into tinfoil boxes like Jules's, pointed up at the sky.

Jules puts his eye to his box. "Nothing yet," he reports.

I'm sixty years old, I think. I don't have this kind of time to waste.

Actually, it occurs to me, I have nothing but time and nothing to do but waste it.

The tumble starts, ears ringing, throat tight. Be here now, I tell myself. Looking for distraction, I scan the canyon in front of me, dotted with houses clinging to dry, golden hillsides. Some are funky, teetering on wooden stilts, faithful to their Laurel Canyon legacy. Others are glassy, modern, post-Joni-era mansions, squatting on massive cement piers. Beyond the iconic skyline of downtown L.A., the Pacific is a glint of silver, lavender smog blanketing the wild swirl of serpentine streets. As I watch, the hot orange orb of the sun sinks to meet the horizon, setting the skyscrapers on fire.

Here I am, someplace new and different. A pulse of excitement flits through me, hummingbird wings beating back my grief.

Days ago I was riding my bike through Berkeley neighborhoods that had long lost their mystery, turning corners, knowing exactly what I would find. I close my eyes now and let the soft breeze warm me. Even since climate change, the Bay Area was never balmy enough for me. Maybe I've accidentally come to exactly the right place.

"It's starting!" Jules hands me the cardboard box. "Look!"

I don't know what an annular eclipse is and I don't care. I lift the box to my eye. Oh, great. As promised, the moon has turned the sun into a gold wedding band.

"Isn't it incredible?" Jules crows.

I swallow hard. "I'm sure it is. I guess I'm just not into astrology."

"Astronomy," Jules corrects me.

"Case in point." Jeez, I chastise myself. This guy's sharing his home with me, trying to share an eclipse with me, and I don't appreciate any of it.

No wonder I'm sixty and sleeping on a stranger's couch.

If I opened my mouth right now and said the truest thing in the truest way, I'd wail like the six-year-old I am inside, exiled to summer camp, sobbing on the phone to my parents, begging them to let me come home.

But this isn't summer camp. This is my actual life.

Also, I'm not six.

Also, there's no one to call.

Also, I don't have a home.

"So beautiful." Jules sighs. At least he didn't let me ruin this for him. I envy him his unfettered delight.

THE SKY GOES INKY. The skyscrapers fade into the night. Jules pulls out a flashlight and the two of us follow the pale yellow circle of light down the hill.

Except for the faint whoosh of cars on Hollywood Boulevard, the night sounds are nature's. Since I left my Taos hippie mountaintop in the 1970s, I've missed hearing crickets and birds chirping their small-town sunset songs. How strange that Los Angeles is the place I get to hear them again.

"Home sweet home." Jules pushes through the unlocked front door.

Across the large living room, a wall of casement windows and French doors opens to the view to the canyon. Multi-patterned dhurrie rugs crisscross the gleaming oak floor. Vintage velvet easy chairs cozy up to a white Spanish fireplace. In front of the windows, a long wooden farm table is set with Provençal linens and charmingly mismatched plates. The kitchen is what every housewares catalogue cover wants to be, wicker baskets and copper bowls hanging from wrought-iron hooks, marble countertops dotted with chunky wooden cutting boards and apothecary jars. Stoveside, a skyline of olive oils, sea salts, and pepper mills awaits a cook.

"It's gorgeous," I say. "Pure Clara."

"She's amazing, isn't she?" I follow Jules's eyes to a daybed near the front windows, surrounded on three sides by massive painted wooden screens.

"Clara put the screens up before she left," he says. "For your privacy."

I stare at the screens, willing my face not to show my disappointment. When Clara said I could sleep on their couch, I'd envisioned that couch in a room with a door. Now I envision Jules walking by me when I'm sleeping, averting his eyes to avoid the sight of me dreaming and drooling. I envision myself pretending to be asleep so I won't see him walking past me in his briefs or his boxers, or whatever the hell men are wearing under their jeans these days.

"Those screens are beautiful," I manage.

"Chinese antiques." Jules beams. "Clara's pride and joy."

It stabs me, remembering my wife lighting up that way when she talked about me.

"Clara told me to make space in the garage so you can use it as your dressing room."

I follow Jules through the kitchen to the garage. We stand silently regarding the stacks of paintings and overflowing cardboard boxes and gardening tools and old chairs and tables in various stages of repair. There isn't room for a dress in here, let alone a dressing room.

"Sorry." Jules shakes his head. "We have so much junk."

"I'll make it work," I say. "It's so nice of you to put up with me." If my first few hours in Los Angeles are any indication, I'm going to be doing a whole lot of pretending to be the positive person I am not.

Jules bushwhacks his way through the piles and emerges pushing a half-full rolling garment rack. He shoves the clothes on the rack to one side, leaving a few inches of space on the rod for me.

"Want help unpacking?" he asks.

"Thanks. I'll handle it."

"Holler if you need anything."

Jules goes back into the house, and I start hauling armloads of hangers from my car to the garage. It feels like a week ago that I carried these clothes out of the closet I shared, until a few hours ago, with my wife.

Jules reappears. "How you doing out here?"

"All done."

"Glass of wine?" Jules asks.

Right now I'd give a vineyard to be able to walk into a room with a door that closes and close the door. I need to be alone to cry the way a person with diarrhea needs a bathroom. But I owe Jules. There's only one answer to anything he offers me.

"Sounds good," I lie. "Thanks."

I follow Jules to a turquoise metal bistro table on the deck off the kitchen. The stars of Hollywood twinkle below us, a nighttime skyscape turned upside down. Determined to show Jules

and myself that I'm not too strangled by my own story to be interested in someone else's, I pepper him with questions, imitating
my former, genuinely curious self. Jules tells me about his job as
a physics professor, his brother's upcoming marriage, how much
he misses his wife.

Jules sips his wine. "What about you?" he asks.

If I answer him honestly I might feel better, but he'll know he
has a needy, unstable head case on his hands. If I don't . . .

I don't know what will happen if I don't spill my feelings, because I've never not done that. Wouldn't that be *withholding* from
a guy who's being generous and open with me? Covering up my
embarrassing situation? Concealing the real me?

"It's a long story," I say.

Is that relief or fatigue on Jules's face? "Another time, then,"
he says. He outlines his morning routine: when and where he
shaves and showers, reads his *Los Angeles Times*, eats his oatmeal,
drinks his tea.

"Clara told me you like your solitude in the morning," I say. I
stand up and take my half-full wineglass to the sink. If this were
my house, I'd leave it there until my wife drank it or washed it. I
pour out the wine, wash the glass, dry it, open cabinet doors until
I find its mates, and make room for it on the shelf.

"I'll try not to get in your way."

"Mornings can be hectic," Jules says.

"I can only imagine," I say, speaking literally. Mornings, after-
noons, weekdays, weekends have been all the same to me. I haven't
had a day job since 1992.

"Don't let me keep you." Jules gives me an awkward hug. "If I
don't see you before you leave, break a leg."

But he does see me. Right from where he's sitting. He sees me going to the garage to get undressed, and he sees me padding across the living room in my pink-and-green pineapple-print pajamas. He sees me rearranging Clara's wooden screens so he can't see me climb onto the mattress and turn my back to him and pretend to sleep.

I've never understood why some people choose to live alone. I get it now. What a luxury to be able to sleep in one's own home when grief and exhaustion demand it; to be able to speak only when and with whom one wants to speak.

As soon as I hear Jules go downstairs and close the door to his and Clara's bedroom, I reach into the small suitcase I've shoved under the daybed and pull out my itty-bitty book light and my copy of *A Three Dog Life* by Abigail Thomas, a memoir about the end of her happy marriage.

In most books I've found on the subject of marital heartbreak, including Thomas's, the wrenching apart comes with illness or death, not the unexpected, inexplicable dissolution that took down my wife and me. But Abigail Thomas is one of the few writers I've found who's both older than I am and writing about it with utterly believable candor. When my marriage started coming undone, reading Thomas's memoirs one by one became my research project, investigating the possibility of hope.

"I put a life together," Thomas writes of the period following the accident that broke her husband's brain and their life together. "I learned to make use of the solitude I now had aplenty . . . I made new friends, I learned to knit, I met other writers, and we began to get together to share our work."

I close the book and close my eyes, trying to visualize myself making new friends or knitting or meeting other writers. I used to knit, but I can't imagine growing a lapful of wool or wearing anything made of wool in this climate. I used to share my work with other writers, but I can't imagine having the emotional wherewithal to go out and meet writers, let alone write, let alone share my writing.

Footsteps from downstairs make my eyes fly open, jerk my body into full alert. Everything around me is strange: the shadows, the scents, the sounds. That damn six-year-old inside me is wailing *I just want to go home.*

A breeze wafts in through the open windows. It's softer, warmer than the thin, chill Bay Area air. I inhale its jasmine scent. A nearby neighbor's fountain is burbling; a bird is warbling in the dark. I'm not in "Oaktown" anymore. I don't hear couples on the street arguing angrily, police cars in hot pursuit. I don't hear sirens or gunshots or the roaring engines of muscle cars. The few cars that pass by move slowly, silently. I imagine a parade of Priuses ambling along the crooked streets of Laurel Canyon, mountain lions prowling the urban jungle under the light of the moon.

I wonder what my wife is doing, if she's moved out of the guest room and into our bed. Her bed now. Not ours. I wonder if I'll make friends ever again, or knit or write.

Thank you, Ambien: sleep comes fast and hard.

I'M AWAKENED BY A RUMBLE. A crash.

"Earthquake," I try to shout. The sound gets stuck in my throat. I try to run. My legs won't move.

A man's worried face appears at the foot of my bed. "Are you okay?" Jules asks.

Oh, right. I'm in his living room.

I don't live in my house anymore.

I live in L.A.

I can't move my legs.

Jules turns on a lamp. One of the wooden screens is lying across my legs. My right knee pokes through a splintered hole.

Jules lifts the screen off of me, leans it against the wall. "Can you move your leg?"

I hoist myself up onto my elbows and I see that another screen fell, too, but in the opposite direction. It's taken out a few posts from the stairway banister, which now tilts drunkenly into the room.

"Oh my God," I say. "I'm so sorry. I'll—"

I'll what? Ask for a layaway plan to pay for all this destruction?

"I'm sorry," Jules says. "It's not your fault. You probably kicked them over in your sleep. Those screens were tipsy. I'm just glad you're okay."

Those screens, I'm guessing, are—were—worth more than I'll earn in the next six months. Not to mention how much Clara loved them. She has a lot of things, but she cherishes each one.

"Party's over. Let's get some sleep." Jules turns off the lamp and goes downstairs. I hear him close the door to his room.

A sob, barbed with self-pity, rips through my chest. I stuff my face into the pillow, tell myself not to cry. Swollen red eyes is not the look I'm going for on my first day of work.

"Please, God," I whisper, "tell me I'll be okay."

WHEN I WAS A CHILD, bedtime was the worst hour of each day. I was terrified of sleep—of death, really. I didn't trust that my eyes, once closed, would ever open again.

Each night I delayed the inevitable for hours, reading under the covers, my Ringling Bros. circus flashlight trained on the pages of the books I dog-eared again and again: *Little Women*, biographies of Helen Keller and Amelia Earhart, *Betty and Veronica* comics. (Archie and Reggie were idiots, I decided early on.)

One night, at age six or seven, I found a poem called "The Lord's Prayer" on the back cover of my comic book, where the ads for Sea-Monkeys and X-ray glasses were usually displayed. The child of devoutly atheist Jews, I didn't know who "the Lord" was, but the poem seemed written for me.

Now I lay me down to sleep
I pray the Lord my soul to keep
And if I die before I wake
I pray the Lord my soul to take.

It wasn't just me! Whoever wrote the poem was worried about dying before *she* woke, too. This news was a big step toward my seven-year-old salvation. I wanted more of whatever protection this Lord thing offered. I memorized the poem, and every bedtime from that night on, after my mother had turned out the lights, I stood on my tiptoes in the middle of my bed, reached my arms up toward Heaven (where God lives, after all; why would you get on your knees on the *floor*?), and recited that prayer out loud.

The sound of my voice talking to God made me feel like I was keeping track of Him and He was keeping track of me. That way He would know when I died before I waked, and He wouldn't take my soul too early or too late. It was easy to imagine, and I imagined it often. At just the right moment, God would reach down from Heaven and tuck my soul into a plump pink feather bed floating on a fluffy white cloud.

Ending up in a feather bed in Heaven wasn't as good as not dying at all. But it was a whole lot better than dying without knowing where my soul might end up.

Once I'd put God in charge, I started sleeping better. And so was born my foul-weather faith, which persists to this day. Who calls on God during good times? Not me. We've been out of touch for years. But tonight: "Please, God. Tell me this isn't the end of my story. Tell me this isn't what I deserve."

I feel Him lift me up and lay me down on that plump pink feather bed. Relief warms the region of my heart.

"Tell me it'll be okay, God. Someday. Somehow."

I wait. I listen. I hear nothing but my own words echoing in my head.

And then it goes quiet inside me. And in that silence I hear something. Sense something. Think something. Whatever it is, it makes me put my arms around my rigid body and tell myself that it'll be okay. Someday. Somehow.

IT'S A LONG FIRST NIGHT for me in the City of Angels. But when my alarm goes off in the morning, I have something I didn't have the night before. A connection with someone or something I can talk to. Someone or something that gathered me in and held me together when pieces of me started flying around the room. I know there's more falling apart in my future. When it happens, maybe that someone or something will gather me in again.

"Morning," Jules calls from the hallway, alerting me that he's on approach.

"Please, God," I pray, "be with me today."

I swear I intuit or hear or feel something. A reassurance. A vow.

I sit up, throw the covers off my scraped-up legs. "Morning, Jules," I say. "I'll be out of your way soon."

THREE

When I emerge from my garage dressing room, Jules is sitting at the dining table as promised, hunched over his cereal bowl, turning the pages of the *Los Angeles Times*. "I'm off. Have a good day," I say.

"You too," Jules says without looking up.

I linger, hoping for a few words of commute-advice—a shortcut, a commendation for leaving so much time to go such a short distance, the best place to stop for coffee. Jules doesn't offer. I don't ask.

No problem, I tell myself, climbing into my car. Siri and I will persevere. Google Maps said it would take twenty minutes to drive the 3.7 miles from Laurel Canyon to Hollywood and Vine. I'm allowing an hour and fifteen. I'll get within a few blocks of the office, stop for a molto-mega-gigundo-grande latte, and arrive at my new job early, confident, and caffeinated.

Sure enough, I'm one of few cars on Lookout Mountain Avenue. Turning onto Wonderland, I hit a snafu. Clearly Google

Maps didn't account for morning drop-off at Wonderland Avenue School, a bumper-to-bumper lineup of BMW and Mercedes SUVs inching forward to park and discharge their nattily attired tots.

I check the dashboard clock. So far it's taken me fifteen minutes to travel three blocks.

Laurel Canyon Boulevard is congested but moving. Maybe I'll keep my new job after all. Building on this positive moment, as my ex-therapist encouraged me to do, I inventory the good things that lie ahead.

Bellissima is a $50-million-and-growing fashion company: socially and environmentally responsible, seemingly fun-focused and cool. I've been doing some of the company's copywriting since my magazine work dried up, and I liked the staffers I've worked with over the phone. By quitting time today, I will have met at least twenty hip people in Los Angeles, and they'll have met me. Can after-work drinks, girlie shopping sprees, and weekend pool parties be far behind?

No more laboring in freelance isolation. I'll be collaborating with stylish, smart colleagues, producing cutting-edge, high-budget marketing campaigns.

I've excelled at this work before. I know I can do it again—as long as I can keep my evil twin under wraps and limit my grief attacks to nonworking hours.

In our pre-employment negotiations, my boss-to-be, Heather Leong, agreed to the ten-hour, four-day workweeks I proposed. I'll have Fridays off and I'll work at home on Mondays, so I can keep some semblance of a writing life and earn some freelance income to support my personal economic recovery campaign.

When I lost my domestic partner, my monthly health insurance premium went from $600 to nearly $800. From now on that exorbitant necessary expense will be pillaging my employer's pockets, not mine.

I'll have cash money. Deposited in my checking account. Every other week. No more hours spent chasing my freelance checks.

And I'll have perks. Bellissima is the twenty-first-century version of the groovy companies I worked for in the 1980s and early 1990s—Banana Republic, Ben & Jerry's, Odwalla, Smith & Hawken. I'm predicting fun field trips, brainstorming sessions, employee sample sales, and a steady supply of treats supplied by vendors and/or cookie-baking coworkers. Plus all those benefits that freelancers bust their butts to pay for but employees sit back and enjoy: an ergonomic office; the latest, greatest computer; air conditioning when it's hot and heat when it's not; the occasional free lunch, holiday party, weekend retreat.

I still have thirty minutes to get to the office. It couldn't possibly take thirty minutes to drive two miles, could it?

I'm starting to wonder. I wait in place through one green light, advance one car length through the next. Swallowing dread, I check out the scene around me, soothing myself with a noncatastrophic scenario, another one of my therapist's tips. Raised by first-generation staticky, black-and-white TV, I've always been fascinated by Hollywood lore, and look where I am right now: dead center, iconic Hollywood. Outside the passenger window, the historic Roosevelt Hotel, where Marilyn spent her first two years in Los Angeles and had her first photo shoot. On my left, Grauman's Chinese Theatre, the Hollywood Walk of Fame, the Dolby Theatre, where the Oscars are held.

The Oscars! People come from all over the world and pay fifty bucks to ride tour buses past these sights, and I'll be seeing them on my way to work every day, for free. I imagine the Golden Age greats walking the red carpet on this very boulevard, paparazzi lights flashing. A squiggle of excitement worms through my worries. Marilyn left her handprints in that courtyard! Charlton Heston! Lana Turner! Myrna Loy!

Wait. It's 8:40. If the traffic doesn't start moving this minute, I'm going to be late to my first day of work.

I call Celia, an L.A. native, hoping she'll steer me to a shortcut, but her voice mail picks up. I ask Siri for her advice instead, then wonder if they're strict about hands-free driving in L.A. All I need now is a moving violation. I have a great argument for the cops: I'm not driving, I'm parked on Hollywood Boulevard with my engine running. Siri tells me to stay on Hollywood to Vine. She shows my arrival time as 9:15, fifteen minutes after I'm due.

I cannot lose this job. There's got to be faster way. At the corner I take a left, then a right. It's 8:45. It's less congested on the side streets, but there's a stop sign on every corner. Suddenly the street I'm on merges into another and I'm driving in the wrong direction—west instead of east, or is it north instead of south?

Why is there no public transportation in this town? I could be on BART right now, whizzing below the bay.

Why didn't I leave an extra half hour to get to work on my first day?

Is there nothing I can do right?

IT'S 9:40 WHEN I PULL into the Bellissima parking lot. All but one
of the employee parking spaces is occupied. I guess that would
be mine.

I reapply the lipstick I bought yesterday, gather up my brand-
new briefcase and the skirt of my brand-new dress. A short, smiling man appears, opens my car door, and holds it for me.

"*Buenos días, señora,*" he says, extending his hand. "*Yo soy
Juan.*"

"*Mucho gusto,* Juan. I'm Meredith." I don't have time to tell
Juan that I'm no one's señora. I'm focused on getting my ass into
the three-story brick building next door, where I was due forty-
two minutes ago.

Juan gestures at my road-weary car. "Your car is very dirty. I
detail for you?"

"Sure," I say. "Thanks."

Wondering what this red-carpet car wash is going to cost me,
I sprint toward Bellissima's frosted-glass doors, punch in the
alarm code that came with my offer letter, and burst into the
glass-brick-lined entryway. Sweat drips down my back, the backs
of my legs, my freshly made-up face.

My face! I race to the women's bathroom, dab at my raccoon
eyes with a paper towel, take another precious moment to summon a calming mantra. As I stare at my smeared face and deer-
in-the-headlight eyes, the phrase "Fake it till you make it" springs
to mind.

My mother forced that concept on me in junior high. If I'd just *act as if* I didn't care about the boy who'd dumped me, she said; if I could just *act as if* I cared about passing algebra, eventually the pretense would become real. Rolling my eyes at her "hypocrisy," I'd refuse her, rigid with adolescent self-righteousness.

Now I'm thinking my mother might have been onto something. The stakes are too high to risk being myself. Faking it is the best I can do. Making it is beyond belief.

AS INSTRUCTED, I report to Norma, VP of "Talent Development." If Norma notices the mess of my face or the fact that I'm forty-eight minutes late, she hides it well. She jumps up, grabs me in a hug. "Welcome, Meredith," she bubbles. "We're so happy you're here!"

"Me too." My voice hangs between us, flat and heavy. "So happy!" I chirp, reminding myself that it's true, or at least it should be. I *am* damn lucky to be here.

"Isabel isn't here this week, but I'll introduce you to everyone else."

During our FaceTime interview, Isabella Galliana, the thirty-four-year-old daughter of an Italian model and an American director, had told me that she protects her creativity by staying out of the company's day-to-day operations. She "divides her time," as the celebrity bios say, between L.A. and Milan, working on new designs, keeping her finger on the European pulse. The employee handbook describes Isabel's philosophy as "MBA: Managing by Not Being Around."

I follow Norma through Bellissima headquarters, a renovated button factory, now a showcase of stylish un-improvements—

exposed brick walls, exposed rusty beams, exposed galvanized pipes, exposed stair treads, exposed concrete floors. Skylights, industrial casement windows, and vintage light fixtures make it almost as bright inside as out. Ethnic art hangs on every vertical surface—paintings, textiles, garments, masks of many lands.

"The lunchroom." Norma waves glossy crimson fingernails at a big open space with a family-sized fridge, two microwaves, a purified-water dispenser, a juicer, and an elaborate gleaming espresso machine.

The dining area is centered around a long pine table containing a still life of contemporary takeout culture and its detritus: wrinkled chopstick wrappers, Trader Joe's tikka masala boxes, Chipotle bags, little plastic tubs of satay sauce, glistening kale shreds, and bottles of au courant condiments—sriracha, soy sauce, chutney, Tapatío.

"We're eaters here," Norma says, sweeping the garbage into a tall willow basket.

"I'm an eater, too."

"Then you'll fit right in." Norma beams.

Norma walks me through the departments: Design, Marketing, Customer Service, Sales, Finance. Actual offices line the perimeter of the building; the worker bees sit at spiffy modern workstations, each with a desk, an Aeron chair, a landline phone, and a big-screen iMac. Most of the "team members"—Bellas, in the company vernacular—seem to be using their own cell phones.

The Bellas are a good-looking bunch, glossy haired and sparkly eyed, with bright white straight-toothed smiles. Their good looks and confidence conjure happy childhoods in interesting neighborhoods with interesting moms and dads who gave them their interesting names. I figure I'm ten to twenty years older than most of their parents and—gulp—the same age as the younger Bellas' grandmothers.

"The kids," as I immediately name them, are relaxed and gracious, greeting me as if Bellissima was their company and hiring me was their decision. For all I know, it was. Isabel calls her company "an employee-centered workplace." Maybe it's true.

The whole groovy package would make Bellissima my perfect reentry job, except for one tiny thing (my coworkers) and one medium-sized thing (me). I haven't worked in a bra or a waistband in twenty-two years, when both bra and waistband were much smaller. Most of the Bellas are so young, so lean, and so drop-dead gorgeous, the place looks more like a modeling agency waiting room than a fashion company's office. As I'm being introduced to a sweet girl named Marguerite—tall, willowy, with wavy red hair to her wasp waist—I catch a reflection of the two of us in a full-length mirror. Mortified, I resolve to avoid repeating that experience.

With each Bella I meet, my belly looks bigger to me, my wrinkles deeper, my hair, makeup, and first-day-of-work outfit lamer. By the time Norma leaves me with Heather—my thirtysomething, Bellissima-minidress-and-Gucci-bootie-wearing boss—I'm hoping my employee benefit package includes unlimited plastic surgery and a burial plot.

I'm aware that this is a thing, and I'm aware that the thing is bigger than I am. Ten thousand Americans turn sixty-five every day. Thanks to modern medicine, our massive consumption of kale, and the "we're here to redefine everything" attitude of those of us who came of age in the 1960s, retirement isn't on our iCals.

While we're clutching our careers with our cold, dying hands, the kids are gamboling past us. In workplaces everywhere, people my age are getting pats on the (aching) back and performance reviews from people Heather's age.

I should be used to it. In the past twenty years, I've suddenly found myself older than my doctors, my editors, my therapists, my mortgage broker, and most of my friends. But this is different. I'll be coming to this office three days a week every week, until I'm too old to shuffle in here anymore. What was I thinking, moving to a city famous for worshiping wealth and beauty and youth?

I follow Heather to my office. It's a spacious, light-flooded room with curved glass-brick walls, midcentury-modern bookshelves, a gray flannel easy chair, and two gray melamine desks. "That's you," Heather says, pointing at one of them. She points to the other. "Our social media person, Charlotte, sits there."

So I'll be sharing a room with a stranger all day, then sharing a house with a stranger all night. At least there's the car. I'll have two hours a day alone, three days a week, getting to work and back.

"Take your time settling in," Heather says. "I'll circle back to you in a bit."

I sink into my lumbar-supported Aeron chair and start opening drawers to see what my twenty-six-year-old predecessor left behind. There's only one file drawer in my desk, and that drawer contains no files, just a beat-up copy of the employee handbook and a dented box of Kleenex. Looks like the paperless office, a Jetsons' fantasy when I last had a job, has become a Flintstones reality.

"You must be Meredith." A stunning blonde walks into the

room, drops her beige cashmere poncho and silver leather tote onto the gray flannel chair, and smiles, really smiles, at me. Her streaked golden hair, hazel eyes, and olive skin remind me of the heroine of my beloved childhood chapter books, *Honey Bunch and Norman.*

"I'm Charlotte," she says. "How's your first day going so far?"

I feel an instant connection with Charlotte. For one thing, she's obviously older than the other Bellas, maybe close to forty. And the frame on her desk holds a black-and-white photograph of two little blond boys who look just like her.

Ah. Charlotte's a mom. So she knows love, the deepest love, and she knows worry and vulnerability and pain. Despite our obvious differences, we're members of the same club.

"You okay?" Charlotte asks, squinting at me, sounding as if she actually wants to know.

Horrifyingly, a sob escapes my mouth. Without hesitation Charlotte gets up, walks over to me, and puts her arm around my shoulders. She smells faintly of good *parfum.* She smells like my wife.

"Sorry," I croak. "I'm not usually like this. I mean, lately I *am* like this, but not . . . I'm going through a divorce."

Charlotte gives my shoulders a quick squeeze, then returns to her chair. She folds her hands in her lap, her eyes and her attention trained on me. I can't believe this is happening on my first day on the job. I can't believe how compassionately Charlotte is dealing with it.

"I signed my divorce papers three months ago," she says quietly. "I'm the one who ended it, but still . . ." She sighs. "Still. There's so much pain."

"There is," I say. "So much pain."

"My boys are with their dad this weekend," Charlotte says. "Maybe you and I can have a glass of wine on Friday night."

"I'd love that," I say.

At the same moment Charlotte adds, "Unless you have other plans."

She smiles. I smile.

My aching heart sprouts angel wings. I feel God right next to me, a beaming, loving face inside a brilliant yellow sun.

Thank you, I pray.

FOUR

'm writing hang-tag copy, second day on the job, when Heather appears in the office I share with Charlotte.

"Did anyone tell you to wear your Lulus tomorrow?" my boss asks me. It's 4:30 p.m., and Heather, who arrived at ten this morning, is on her way out the door. Heather is one of several Bellissima employees who live on the Westside, a sixty-to-ninety-minute commute in the morning and a ninety-minute commute in the afternoon.

"Got it," I lie. Heather gives me the thumbs-up and disappears.

"Lulus?" I ask Charlotte.

"Lululemons," Charlotte says. "Tomorrow's Workout Wednesday."

"Which means . . . ?"

"Every Wednesday and Friday morning at nine-thirty, Isabel's personal trainer comes into the office to train us for an hour. It's too much hassle to change, so we all wear Lulus on those days."

My jaw drops. "The whole company comes to work in spandex twice a week? And everyone stops working for an hour to *work out*?"

Charlotte laughs. She must be a recent immigrant, too. I've noticed that the La-La things that seem weird to me also seem weird to her. "Exactly," she says. "It's optional, but most everyone does it."

"*Why?*" I say. "Who in this company needs to get any thinner? Besides me, I mean?"

"You look great," Charlotte says reflexively, the way a hot young thing with a kind heart speaks to a slightly overweight old thing with a bit of a potbelly. "But if you do lose weight, you have a chance to win the fat contest."

"Excuse me?"

"Every three months Joanne weighs and measures us. Whoever loses the most body fat gets a day off with pay."

Charlotte leans across the space between our desks. "Isabel's really into fitness, so . . ." she says.

"Isabel weighs eighty-five pounds." I realize I've spoken a bit louder, perhaps, than I needed to. My voice echoes off the glass-brick wall.

Charlotte laughs again, uncomfortably this time. I realize she probably weighs eighty-eight.

"Do we really have to wear Lululemon?" I ask, hoping I can get away with baggy sweats.

"Of course not," Charlotte says.

My relief fades quickly as I imagine myself working out in my pilly Target sweatpants next to my skinny, fit Lululemon-clad coworkers.

"I have extra Lulus if you want to borrow some," Charlotte says.

"Thanks anyway, but I've been meaning to get a pair," I lie. At $98, Lulu yoga pants weren't at the top of my list. But they are now.

AT NINE-THIRTY THE NEXT MORNING, Joanne bounces into the office. "I'm heeere!" she hollers, the duffel bag she's lugging and her voice outsizing her five-foot frame. Like children in a Pied Piper trance, my coworkers, fitted out in Lulu running bras and skintight shorts and sparkling clean Nikes in matching hallucinatory hues, follow Joanne into the Bellissima warehouse. My butt, in please-make-me-invisible basic black, brings up the rear.

Joanne points her Apple remote at a bank of electronics on a rickety table. Music of a genre I cannot even name blasts into the cavernous room. "Give me twenty push-ups," Joanne barks over the din. Everyone drops to the concrete floor.

I tell myself I can do it. I *have* to do it, even though this is not the kind of workout I did at my Berkeley gym, where the first drop of sweat was my signal to stop, sit down, and have a cold drink. I'm used to "an hour of exercise" that starts with a fifteen-minute warm-up and ends with a fifteen-minute cooldown, interrupted by a brief period of moderate effort.

There is no warm-up today, and I suspect the cooldown will take place at my desk. This is a Los Angeles workout, designed to build the kind of movie-billboard bodies that tower over Sunset Boulevard. This is a solid hour of burpees and crunches and rock climbers interspersed with runs around the block, followed by pull-ups using TRX straps hooked to the front of the building—which happens to be located on Hollywood Boulevard. This makes it extra-convenient for truckers driving by to blast their air horns while leering at my coworkers' perfect bodies.

I make it through the hour, barely, by walking while the others are running, and collapsing onto my stomach, panting, when they're doing push-ups, and "kicking" an inch into the air when they shoot their delicate ankles Rockette-high.

Even worse than my red-hot, sweat-drenched face and shaking legs is the comparing and contrasting I'm doing in my head. I can't seem to keep my eyes from darting back and forth between my crepey cleavage and my female coworkers' perky breasts; between my waggling arms and their chiseled pecs. Even the few men in the group are younger, tighter, and prettier than I am.

After a "run" around the block, I stumble back into the warehouse minutes behind the others. "Good job, Meredith!" Joanne shouts. I duck my head, pleased and embarrassed until I realize that the only other person Joanne compliments is the lone overweight woman in the room.

"I do one-on-one training at the Silverado gym, you know," Joanne says as I pass her on my way to the shower line. "You could get a lot out of it. You're naturally athletic, but you could be a lot more toned."

"Great to know," I say, my humiliation complete.

THE NEXT MORNING, sore and shaky, I limp into my first big Bellissima meeting, a planning session for New York Fashion Week.

Members of the Finance, Marketing, Product Development, Design, and Creative "teams" are sitting around an enormous walnut burl table, swiveling lazily on cushy chairs. I'm here because I'll be writing the press releases, the copy for the booth displays, and Isabel's speech for the show.

The vibe is mellow, a group of friends hanging out, snacking on wasabi seaweed, drinking grass-green juices from the fresh-pressed juicery down the street and water from mason jars, dissecting last night's *Game of Thrones*. "It's a perfect second-date show," Charlotte's boss, Jade, says. "I watched it with this guy I met on Tinder. I learned a lot about him, fast."

"Hey, guys. What's up?" Isabel's image comes to us nearly life-sized from the huge flat-screen on the wall.

Isabel is gorgeous beyond all reason, with a face the screen loves and long, flowing, beach-wavy streaked blond hair. Like her employees, Isabel radiates charm and positivity, but with a fierce gleam in her eyes.

The people around the table greet their boss casually, affectionately. "What are you wearing, Is?" the design director asks, squinting at the screen. "Is that dress ours?"

Isabel grins. "It will be. As soon as Jim figures out how to get it made for a margin we can love."

"Or as soon as Isabel figures out how to get it made in a less politically correct fabric that we can actually afford," says Jim, the Finance VP.

I perk up. Making products that are good for the bottom line *and* good for the world might be a new challenge for Bellissima, but it's a time-honored one for me. Isabel sought me out because

I consulted with Ben & Jerry's and other progressive companies during the 1980s, the heyday of "doing well by doing good." Maybe there's something I can contribute here.

"Hey, Meredith." Isabel flashes me a brilliant smile from the screen. "So happy you're here." She directs her gaze at the group. "Meredith did that awesome direct-mail campaign I told you about. We're lucky to have her."

"I remember reading about that campaign in *Ad Week*," Heather says. "How long ago was that again?"

Was that a dig? "Nineteen ninety-three," I say. "But I've done a few other campaigns since then." I hope I don't sound as lame as I feel.

"You know we're going after the Eileen Fisher market," Isabel says. "I'm hoping Meredith will help us with that. Let's give our new Bella an awesome welcome."

Despite Isabel's casual categorization based solely on my age—my style runs about four decades behind my years, more Forever 21 than Eileen Fisher—I *like* this woman. She's warm and sparkly. I can see us working together well. "Happy to be here," I say, over a limp smattering of applause.

"So, Heather," Isabel says, "what's on your list?"

"Fabrics for the fall line," says Marguerite, the design director, a thirtysomething brunette. "At the last retreat we set a goal of becoming the 'eco-chic innovator.' So I asked the reps to find me something super green and new." She passes her iPad around the table, showing us the swatches on the screen. "They came up with organic bamboo. It's sustainably harvested and produced. It feels like silk, and it's washable. The colorways aren't quite as strong as I'd like, but if our order's big enough, they'll do custom colors for us."

"What's the bad news?" Jim asks.

"You mean, what's the *growthful challenge*?" Isabel teases him.

"The usual," Marguerite says. "Bamboo's twice as expensive as organic cotton. Which of course is twice the price of conventional cotton. Using the bamboo, even for just a few styles, might kick our price points higher than I feel comfortable with."

"But it's awesome fabric!" Isabel says.

"With a great backstory!" Jade chimes in.

"Is anyone else using it?" Heather asks.

"Not that we know of," Marguerite says. "But . . ."

To the young people in this room, the challenge of branding a conscious, caring business in an unconscious, uncaring marketplace is something shiny and new, a puzzle they're being paid well to solve. To me, it's one of many legacies of the sixties movements that changed the world, however incompletely, and made me and their parents—and their grandparents?—who we are.

I want to ask if they're aware of the progenitor of their eight-dollar-a-bottle fresh-pressed juices. That would be the back-to-the-land hippies, including me. Do they know who was "reducing, recycling, reusing" decades before they were gleams in their stoned parents' (or grandparents') eyes?

Uh-oh. I feel the stirrings of bitterness in my belly. The familiar metallic taste of judgment in my mouth.

Since I agreed to take this job I've been warning myself not to make the mistakes that have made me pretty much unemployable for most of my adult life. I know I need to listen more than I talk. Collaborate, not control. Stay open to my coworkers' points of view. In other words, show a little respect for my fellow beings— an attitude at odds with the defensive, self-protective disdain I learned at my Jewish forebears' knees.

"So," Isabel is saying, "we'll use the hemp fabric for five SKUs and organic cotton for the others. And we'll go with the good caterer, but we'll set up a buffet instead of shelling out for servers. Everyone cool with that?"

There's something about Isabel's smile, her humility, her humor that seems to work like kryptonite on my dark side. For an instant I catch a glimpse of her, and my coworkers, and even myself, in a softer light.

Maybe being young and attractive doesn't make the Bellas' sense of mission and discovery one bit less earnest or innocent or sincere than my own and my colleagues' was forty years ago.

Maybe there's more than one spot in history for a generation to be pioneering in its time. Maybe it was our turn in the sixties, and it's the millennials' turn now. Maybe every generation gets to have the same thoughts, invent the same ideas, for the first time.

Contemplating this, I'm surprised to feel my anger dissipating and my heart lifting.

Going around the table, each Bella gives her or his assent.

When they get to me, I say, "I'm in."

ON FRIDAY, I'm lying on the couch on Jules's deck, Googling "moving on from grief."

Of the 92,100,000 results, most seem to revolve around Elisabeth Kübler-Ross's five stages, which I memorized thirty-five years ago in the terrible months following the sudden death of my fifty-eight-year-old mother-in-law. Attempting to situate myself, now, on the continuum of denial/anger/bargaining/depression/acceptance, I realize that I've been pinballing through four of the five stages each day.

Denial helps until I realize that I'm in it, and that realization plunges me into depression—deep sadness, really; I've been depressed, so I know the difference. Bargaining is on a loop in my head. "If I pray every night, if I stay late at work, if I brake instead of accelerate at the next yellow light . . ." Bargaining sometimes ends in anger at myself for being such an idiot. Acceptance seems light (dark) years away.

As usual, I find wisdom in poetry—in this case, Mary Oliver's "In Blackwater Woods." She says that to live in this world, you must be able to love what is mortal; and, when the time comes, to let it go.

Much as I deny it, rage against it, bargain with God about it, or get depressed about it, I know that the time has come to let it go. Unfortunately, knowing that it's time to let go of my mortal love doesn't make it one bit easier to do.

CHARLOTTE TEXTS ME A LINK to a West Hollywood bistro that meets her criteria—outdoor seating, within a couple of miles of the Bellissima office—and mine, happy-hour discounts on drinks *and* food. Instantly, I'm lifted, looking forward to my first L.A. friendship date. My friends from "back home" are doing a great job of buoying me up by phone, but I'm desperate for a face-to-face connection.

I offer to pick Charlotte up, since the office is on my way from Jules's house to the bar. Charlotte texts back: *In LA everyone drives own car. Always. Everywhere. #carpool #rookiemove. See u @5.*

At five we're texting each other again because we're separately stuck in epic traffic, even by L.A. standards. At five forty-five we're texting each other again because we're prowling the same five-block radius, looking for a place to park. At six-fifteen, we're ordering martinis (me), Pinot Grigio (Charlotte), and five-dollar ahi sliders and truffle fries, bonding over the tandem traffic battle we just fought.

Looking around the densely packed sidewalk café, I notice a preponderance of rainbows. Two men, otherwise naked, are wearing matching rainbow bikinis and matching rainbow flip-flops. The woman at the next table has rainbow-painted fingernails and toes. The elderly gentleman at the edge of the patio is holding a rainbow-dyed teacup poodle.

"Special occasion?" I ask our tall, handsome waiter. He laughs as if we're all in on the joke, and whirls off to get our drinks.

The exquisitely styled Lady Gaga impersonator at the adjoining table leans in close, her platinum wig brushing my arm. "Happy Pride!" she (or possibly he) says.

"Pride?" Charlotte says.

"You must be from out of town. Well, you ladies lucked out," Gaga bubbles. "Tonight's the first night of Gay Pride weekend. Half a million people are on their way to this very spot as we speak. And you have front-row seats!"

"But it's only June eighth," I say. "Pride is the last weekend in June."

"In lesser locales, yes," Gaga says, batting her inch-long

rainbow-colored eyelashes. "But, darlin', you're in the City of Angels now. We're always ahead of the curve." She giggles, grabs her overflowing breasts, and gives them a shake. "So to speak."

I turn to Charlotte. "So . . . you and I arranged to meet on the gayest corner of the gayest city on the gayest night of the year."

As Charlotte takes this in, I realize I'm assuming she's straight. And that she's probably assuming the same of me. God, are you listening? Please make it okay with Charlotte that I'm gay.

"The person I'm getting divorced from is a woman," I tell her. "I've been going to San Francisco Pride parades for the last twenty-five years. I should have known better."

"Talk about your rookie moves," Charlotte says without hesitation. "No *wonder* it took us an hour to park."

This strikes me as funny. So funny that something strange happens. I laugh. I laugh! Charlotte laughs, too.

I take a long sip of my pretty basil martini, put the pretty glass down.

"Did you hear that?" I blurt. "I just said the D word and *laughed*."

"Congratulations." Charlotte raises her goblet, and we clink glasses. "To laughter," she says. "Whenever, wherever, whyever."

How committed would I have to be to my misery to let it blind me to all this color, all this pride, all these bright spirits, all this fun? Apparently, more committed than I am. And so, for a couple of hours on the first night of my first Los Angeles Gay Pride weekend, I experience my first sustained break from years of relentless despair.

When I return to the spot where I left my car and find it missing, and walk around looking for it elsewhere in case I misremembered its location, and return to the spot where I parked it and find it still missing, and carefully read the four seemingly contradictory signs on the nearest pole, and I realize that the gay City of West Hollywood has towed my car, and I call an Uber to take me to the tow yard, where I write a check for $250, it barely puts a dent in my greatly improved mood. Somehow, I landed in one of the world's greatest, gayest cities. Better yet, I have a friend who lives there, too.

FIVE

Memorial Day weekend. For the first time in decades I'm being paid not to work. Unfortunately, four days without adult supervision is not my idea of fun right now.

Jules goes east to meet up with Clara, so at least my pity party goes unwitnessed—even by God, who seems to have taken the long weekend off. S/He doesn't respond to my prayers for a call from Charlotte, a knock on the door from a neighbor, an invitation from anyone for anything. Various sub-cliques of my co-workers, according to their Facebook posts, are hanging out together, showing off their bikini bods at pool parties, toasting one another at bars, playing Frisbee at Zuma Beach. Of course they don't invite me to join them; I wouldn't have invited someone my age when I was theirs. So I spend my first paid day off in a couple of decades in a borrowed bed beneath wide-open windows, listening to other people's laughter, smelling other people's grilling food.

When the infernal sunlight finally dims, I seek comatose

comfort, bingeing on Prosecco and *Sex and the City* reruns, telling myself I'm crying because Aidan broke up with Carrie. I mean, Carrie at Miranda's wedding, bravely wiping away tears, mustering a smile for her bestie's wedding photos? Who wouldn't cry at *that*?

I have big social plans for Saturday. I'm going to waylay the mailman, just to make sure my voice still works. While taking a ninety-second pee break from my stakeout, I hear the mail slithering through the slot, plopping onto the floor. Opportunity missed.

By the time the weekend is finally over, I've committed a host of inglorious firsts. First Trader Joe's frozen meal. First bottle of bubbly consumed alone. First holiday with no human contact. First holiday without a home.

MY FIRST PAYCHECK CARRIES good news and bad. Given deductions, it's going to take months to save enough money for first and last months' rent. And then there will be furnishing my new place from scratch, since scratch is what I currently own. I'm going to have to supplement my income with some freelance work. At least I've got plenty of time to do it, what with all these empty nights and weekends.

I e-mail Pam, a bestselling writer friend who's always fielding editing requests from the would-be authors who flock to her events. Twenty minutes after I ask her to send any surplus work my way, I get an e-mail from "Kenny Loggins." Spam, I assume, and hit delete. Then my phone rings.

"Meredith? This is Kenny Loggins. I just turned sixty, and I want to write a book about my life. Pam said you could help."

———

THREE DAYS LATER, Kenny and I are sitting on the patio of his Los Olivos mountaintop compound, overlooking a green meadow wrapped around a turquoise pool. Kenny Loggins is telling me the stories of his life. As he talks, I'm typing into my laptop, sketching an outline for his book, falling just the tiniest bit in love. I can't believe this is a work meeting. With a rock star. Whose songs have been the soundtrack of my life.

During a lull, my stomach growls. Kenny laughs, jumps up, and pulls me to my feet. "This day's too pretty for working. And I already know you're the right person for the job. You're hired, okay? Let's go have lunch on the beach."

The two of us and Barney, Kenny's Australian shepherd, climb into a hybrid SUV. Kenny opens the sunroof as we head down the mountain. The sky above the beckoning sea is even bluer than L.A.'s. The air is crisp and ocean-kissed and clean.

Kenny takes a hand off the wheel, slips a disc into the CD player. "I have a new band. Our first album's dropping this fall. Want a taste?"

"Sure," I say. Pinch me, I think.

The car fills with sweet, sad guitar strains and a woman's voice, singing about being alone on a Friday night after a breakup. Kenny joins in, his voice in the car entwining with his voice on the CD.

The sun comes up / It's another day . . . / And you see, Hey, I'm still breathing.

Take it from me / These little victories / Are all a heart needs.

I pretend to look out the window, my vision blurred with tears.

Kenny puts a hand on my shoulder. "It's okay to cry."

Dammit. How does he know?

"I felt the sadness in you," he says. "That's why I played you that song."

"How?"

"I've been there. Not so long ago."

Kenny pulls into a beachside parking lot. He snaps a leash onto Barney's collar and takes me by the elbow and walks us to a podium in the sand. "Nice to see you, Mr. Loggins," says the maître d', who's wearing a T-shirt and cutoffs. He leads us past the line of people waiting for a table and sweeps us into front-row seats. Twenty feet away, the Pacific roars and swallows the beach and spits it out again.

"Kick your shoes off, Meredith," Kenny says. "Curl your toes in that nice warm sand."

The waiter appears. He puts a glass of ice water in front of Kenny and a brimming golden margarita in front of me. "They have the best blood-orange margaritas here," Kenny says.

"You're not having one?" I want to chug my drink, but I'm attempting grace.

Kenny shakes his head. "I had too much fun in my younger days. My drinking days are done."

The waiter returns with a brightly painted plate of shrimp tacos, a terra-cotta bowl of guacamole, a Mexican basket of chips. Kenny swallows a taco in two bites.

"You feel like talking about it?" he asks me.

Of course I do. I always feel like talking about it. But never more than in this moment, because I have more than a little bit of a crush on this sweet, handsome man, and because I'm sure this whole day is a dream. So I tell Kenny Loggins my story. And then I look up and somehow I've finished my margarita, and Barney's silky, heavy head is in my lap, and somehow we've eaten every bite of food on the table, and somehow, somehow, I feel better.

Kenny asks if I have time for a walk on the beach. I have time for anything he has in mind. He bends to unleash Barney. The dog bounds into the ocean, all clumsiness and wild energy and joy.

"I was married to the love of my life, too," Kenny says. "Everyone envied what we had. We even wrote a book about lasting love. When she left me for a young piano player, I was one hundred percent sure that I'd never be happy again."

"And were you?" I ask. "Ever happy again?"

"I'm happy now," Kenny says. He smiles at me. "Very."

My heart races. I open my mouth to say, "I'm happy now, too," but Kenny's still talking.

"I was onstage giving a concert. Sandra was in the front row. I pulled her onto the stage. We've been together ever since." Kenny flips through his phone, shows me a picture of a young, thin, beautiful blonde.

"She's gorgeous," I say around a puckered mouthful of jealousy.

Kenny beams at me, the short gray hairs in his goatee glinting in the afternoon light.

I choke down my disappointment. So this unexpected instant intimacy is not going to come to a love-song conclusion. Still, I had this. This real connection. This magical day.

Barney gallops up to us, matted and panting and drenched. "Watch out," Kenny says. "He's going to—"

He does. Barney does what he was born to do, spraying us with seawater and sand. Laughing, Kenny and I brush ourselves off.

"I'm more in love than I've ever been," Kenny says, slipping his phone into the back pocket of his jeans. "Trust me. Someday you will be, too."

Hope flickers. I don't want hope. I don't want Kenny Loggins or my silly groupie fantasies. All I want is my wife.

WHO KNEW? Summer is lousy with paid holidays. Since Bellissima had a wildly profitable last quarter, and since Isabel believes in sharing the wealth with those who helped create it, we're all getting the whole week of July Fourth off with pay.

Never have I been so filled with dread by the prospect of so much paid time alone. I've got more me-time than I need at my new digs, a midcentury-modern manse clinging to the side of a Studio City hill. I'm cat- and construction-sitting for Karen, a writer I "met" exchanging witticisms on Twitter, back when I was witty and married and fun.

Karen is having a deck built while she's away. Demolition started the day before I arrived. The workers' first move was to remove the steep steps that descended from Karen's front door to the sidewalk twenty feet below.

Some nights I get home in the dark to find the workers have left me a fully outstretched, shaky twenty-foot ladder. Some mornings I climb down "steps" nailed onto plywood sheets. My route from "home" into the world is a lot like my path through

life these days: unpredictable, ever-changing, ranging from difficult to *How the hell am I supposed to do this?*

ON THE EVE of my Independence Day vacation, lying in Karen's
bed wrestling with despair, I call Celia. We talk about what we've
been talking about since I left Oakland, my wife's refusal to take
my calls or answer my e-mails or texts. And then Celia says something she's never said before, in a tone she's never used with me
before, not quite cold but not exactly reeking of warmth.

"She's not doing it to hurt you," Celia says. "She's in pain, too,
you know."

My heart thumps. "How do you know she's in pain?"

Silence.

"Have you talked to her?"

More silence.

"You've been talking to her?" My voice catches. "And you
didn't tell me?"

"I love her," Celia says. "You know that."

But you're supposed to love me more, I think. You chose *me*.

"Why didn't you tell me?" I ask, trying not to cry.

"Because I knew you'd react this way."

"I tell you everything. Are you telling her what I tell you?"

"Of course not."

"What's she saying about me?"

More silence. And then Celia says gently, lovingly, "I can't be
friends with both of you if I tell you that."

"*What?* You're going to be *friends* with her?"

"I'm not sure. She's clearly ambivalent. But I hope so."

The room tilts. I've never been this drunk.

"I get why this is hard for you, honey," Celia says. "But try to be a grown-up, okay? I can love both of you."

"Be a *grown-up*? Did you really just say that?"

"You're proving my point."

In our decades of friendship, Celia and I have never had a fight. I used to get annoyed when she'd invite me over for dinner and take forever to get the meal on the table. I solved the problem by preemptively snacking before I showed up at her place. She used to get mad when I called her too early in the morning. It took years, but she trained me to wait until ten.

"I love you," I manage, "but I can't talk about this right now."

"I understand."

I don't want Celia to *understand*. I want her to apologize and say she'll never speak to my wife again.

"I'll call you tomorrow," she says, and hangs up.

I take an Ambien and pray for quick sleep.

THE NEXT MORNING I wake up in Karen's bed with a crushing load on my chest. The cats? I open my eyes. Leopold and Loeb are glaring at me, as usual, from their towel-draped chair across the room. It must be the weight of my fight with Celia last night.

The blinds are shut tight, but still I know that the sky is cornflower blue, as it always is; the sun is beaming, as it always is. The perfect-weather week snarls at me, teeth sharp, ready to snap. I sit up, determined to push into the day. The cats need food and water, thank God. I pour organic kibble into a bowl set into an elevated contraption that Karen got from her cats' chiropractor to avoid strain on the kitties' necks while they eat and drink.

I had a cat when I was eighteen, living with my boyfriend in a Greenwich Village walk-up. She drank milk from a bowl on the floor. If my cat ever had neck pain, I never knew it. But that was a million years ago, before cats had chiropractors and children were allergic to bread. I try to ignore the stench of the cat box. Can't.

This improves the day's prospects. There's something I need to do. I'll walk to the Petco on Ventura Boulevard, buy kitty litter, and walk back. Depending on the ladder arrangement the carpenter left me last night, my errand could eat up an hour, maybe two.

I need a better time killer. I'll stop at Crossroads, shop for new old clothes. I'll go to Trader Joe's, drink a tiny free cup of their coffee, eat a tiny free sample, pick up a bottle or two of Prosecco for tonight. By the time I get "home," if I walk slowly enough, half the day will be gone. Celia will call me while I'm walking, or I'll call her. We'll make up. I'll feel better then.

I shrug into my backpack, slither through the front door, blocking the cats' escape with my feet. I lock the door, accomplishing the freeloader's mission: keep the cats inside and the burglars out. I climb backward down today's ladder, a combo package of plywood and rope.

I take a few steps along the sidewalk. Something's wrong.

Something's wrong with the day.

Or something's wrong with me.

The sun is so hot. My chest hurts.

Maybe I'm having a heart attack. Maybe not.

Why is the light so bright in my eyes?

My chest feels heavy again, the way it did when I woke up.

Ah. Hello, grief.

I start walking again. It's hard. The heat, the blazing light, the pain in my chest.

You can't have me, grief. I keep walking, pushing through it.

I wish Patricia and Blue could walk me to the pet store.

I wish Patricia hadn't died.

I see a yard-sale sign. The yard sales are so much better here, all those rich, trendy L.A. women purging their throwaway designer outfits. I spend three bucks on a polka-dot butter dish, in case I ever have my own refrigerator again, and a pair of sparkly deco chandelier earrings, and a vintage cotton sundress in case I ever have someplace to go. The dress is French, white with lime-green pinstripes, its cotton so fine it makes my fingertips hum. I can't quite zip it up, but Joanne and I will fix that. I put on the earrings, stuff the dress and the butter dish into my backpack, and continue down the hill.

My new earrings brush against my neck as I walk, almost like a lover's touch.

But the sun. The glare. The earrings are too heavy. They hurt my ears. I take them off, set my backpack on the ground, toss them into the smallest pocket. I don't know why I'm keeping them. They won't hurt any less tomorrow. They're just another mistake in a long line of mistakes.

Like walking to buy kitty litter. Even if it would fit in my backpack, which it won't, I couldn't carry it up this hill. What an idiot I am.

I duck into Trader Joe's. It's so cool and so cheerful in here.

Hand-lettered chalk signs, flowers, a fragrant grind-your-own coffee stand. I remember when TJ's first came to Berkeley. My wife and I loved to rail against its existence. Shrink-wrapped kale in the garden bowl of the world! Frozen ethnic foods in a town bursting with cheap ethnic dives! But then one day I snuck into TJ's and discovered its nut selection, the wonder of its prices. It wasn't my last clandestine visit. It became a stop on my way home: stopping at TJ's for my wife's favorite dark-chocolate-hazelnut bars and my beloved chili-lime cashews, then transferring them, upon my arrival home, into an unlabeled mason jar. Maybe if I'd been less sneaky . . . Maybe that's why . . .

Sinking.

No.

Swim.

Swim.

I find the tasting booth in the back of the store. I slug a mini-cup of Trader Joe's coffee, swallow a one-inch square of warm, buttered cinnamon toast. Next, the wine aisle: two bottles of Vinho Verde. Better make it three.

The mini-jolts of caffeine and sugar do their job. Grateful for the lift, I surf the wave. I'll get the damn kitty litter later, Angeleno style, in my car. Look how cute the checkout stands are, each one named for a different old-school movie star. I choose Susan Hayward. My cashier is so dreadlocky friendly, he actually cheers me up.

My phone rings as I'm exiting the chilled air. Celia, I think. Thank God. But it's Larissa, another San Francisco friend I've known for twenty years. "Just checking in with you," she says. "I know the holidays are hard."

Larissa's voice is as familiar to me as my face. It's weird to hear it here, in a place she's never seen, a place we've never been together. Does she still know *me* if she doesn't know this parking lot, the bearing-down intensity of this heat, this light?

I sink onto a low cement wall and burst into tears. My grief is a living thing, a beast thrashing inside me. In my best moments, I can contain it, deny it, console it, cajole it. But it's roaring now.

"Mer?" Larissa is saying. I can't answer. I'm crying too hard.

A young guy in a tropical Trader Joe's shirt kneels in front of me. "Are you all right, ma'am? Did you fall? Are you hurt?"

Oh, great. Now I look like an old lady who's taken a fall in a store. I shake my head and push myself upright. "Meredith!" Larissa is saying in my ear.

Larissa and I have walked each other through two decades of best and worst and all the minutiae in between: abortion, marriage, cancer scares, infertility, new love, miscarriage, divorce. I handed Larissa her squalling newborn baby daughter. We danced at each other's weddings. We toasted her parents' fiftieth anniversary, my first book deal, her last premarital romance. Larissa loved my wife. She loved us as a couple. Watching our marriage fall apart, she told me once, was like watching someone set the *Mona Lisa* on fire, with no way to put it out.

I hang up the phone. I can't handle any of it. Larissa, four hundred miles away. The fight with Celia, unresolved. The weight of the bottles in my backpack. The weightlessness of me, drifting through this day, this week, this life.

"Ma'am? Do you want to come inside and cool off?" The Trader Joe's kid puts a gentle hand on my elbow.

"No, thanks." Someone has to help me, but not this guy.

Where's my wife? Somewhere being glad I'm not with her, not taking my calls.

I want her anyway. I want Patricia. I want my dad to tell me who I am, who I've always been. I want Celia to call and make up with me.

I gaze at the Pinkberry across the parking lot. I imagine the smooth cold sweet sliding down my throat. When I was four and I had my tonsils taken out, my dad brought me my mother's nightly treat: hand-packed pints of Breyers ice cream. He put me in his bed and fed it to me, spoonful after soothing spoonful.

Maybe the sound of my father's voice will calm me. "He's sleeping, Mer," my stepmother tells me from the other end of the line. Her tone is distracted, upset.

"Is he okay?" I ask.

After a long silence, she answers. "He felt better yesterday. Maybe he'll feel better tomorrow."

"Anything I can do?"

"I'll tell him you called. That will cheer him up."

Usually breathing helps when I get like this. Right now breathing makes it worse. The wine bottles clink against one another in my backpack. Maybe they'll break while I'm walking. I can't breathe. I slump onto a bus-stop bench, forcing air into my lungs. My chest hurts. I didn't get the kitty litter. Did I close the kitchen window? When I get back, will the cats have run away?

My phone rings. "I'm sorry, honey," Celia says.

I take a deep, hot breath. "I'm sorry, too. You were right. I acted like a big baby."

"You're grieving. I know it's hard."

"My chest hurts. And it's so fucking hot."

"Your chest is hot? Or it's hot outside?"

"Both."

"Where are you?" Celia asks.

"In a bus stop. I'm not sure how to get back to where I'm staying."

"Sweetie, the address is in your phone, isn't it? I'll hold on while you get the directions."

Of course. There's an app for that.

"I'll stay on with you till you get home," Celia says.

The thought of that much conversation exhausts me. So does saying no. "Thanks," I say. I squint at the map on my phone, start back up the hill.

"Did something bad happen today?" Celia asks. "Besides our spat, I mean? I've never heard you sound so low."

"Everything bad happens every day," I say. "It hurts to breathe."

"What about . . . you know . . . praying?" Celia asks in the awkward way that my atheist friends, which is to say most of my friends, refer to my renewed relationship with God.

"I don't have it in me to pray." I inhale a ragged breath. "I don't have it in me to keep living like this."

"What does that mean, Meredith?" Celia asks.

"I'm not going to kill myself," I say. "But I have nothing to look forward to except bad things. I don't want to be here anymore."

I wonder if I'm being manipulative, because it helps the tiniest bit to hear Celia say, "Meredith. We love you. We need you here."

"I love you, too. I won't . . . do anything stupid."

"Good," Celia says, and we hang up.

I make my way back to Karen's house, climb the ladder, rummage through the bathroom cabinets for a thermometer. I discover that I have a fever of 102. I climb back down the ladder and drive myself to the ER—my second trip there in the past month. A different doctor tells me I have bronchitis and prescribes a course of antibiotics. Swaying on my feet, weepy with fever and self-pity, I push a cart through a grocery store, buy a chicken and some onions and garlic. Go back to Karen's. Climb the ladder. Make myself a pot of chicken soup.

Is this what the rest of my life will be like? Being so sad that I keep ending up in the ER? Being so alone that I'm making chicken soup for myself?

I thought I had old age nailed. What better quality-of-life insurance could there be than being in love with a woman who's in love with me? I wasn't going to be one of those small-minded, no-life old ladies, driven batty by solitary confinement. So much for insurance. Now I'm even living with cats.

If I'm going to live, I cannot be this alone.

Although I haven't quite given up trying to traverse it, the road to reconciliation with my wife is looking more impassable every day. But friends. Friends, I can make. My Bay Area friends are lifesavers, but I need new friends. Local friends. Because a body in need of solace needs bodies, not just voices crackling through a hard, flat phone pressed against my burning ear.

SIX

The antibiotics kick in. My fever breaks. My chest lightens. So does my heart, knowing that some of my pain, at least, was physical. Determination replaces despair. I need to get myself into therapy. And I need to make some friends in L.A.

The therapy is the easy part. My new health insurance covers twenty-six sessions per year. With fifty-five years of therapy behind me, I'm normally a meticulously selective consumer, but my PPO assigns me a staff therapist, which is fine, since all I need is someone to make sympathetic faces while I cry. Olivia does that for me, and more. She rebuts my self-loathing. ("I don't know why you're blaming yourself for the end of your marriage. It takes two to save a relationship, and it sounds like you did everything you could.") My appointments with Olivia leave me feeling cared about and comforted and known.

Making friends is a tougher job, but it needs doing. In the words of my childhood heroine, Helen Keller, "Walking with a friend in the dark is better than walking alone in the light."

I discovered the joys of bestieness in first grade, sitting next to Gail Lieberman in the PS 187 auditorium, which doubled as our lunchroom, trading my Velveeta with Gulden's mustard on Pepperidge Farm for her squishable purple-stained Philadelphia cream cheese and Welch's grape jelly sandwiches on Wonder Bread, whispering secrets about the mean girls. Since then, friendships have been my best source of fun, camaraderie, adventure, solace, and self-awareness, and my best source of advice about every big and little thing.

"Each friend represents a world in us," Anaïs Nin wrote, "a world not born until they arrive, and it is only by this meeting that a new world is born." I live for those new worlds. I'm a huge fan of falling in love, and falling in friendship love is a kissing cousin of the consuming-lust stage of early romance. A new friendship brings confidences and cocktails and couch-cuddling, and shopping expeditions, and travel. In good times, a hike or a dinner or a movie with a friend is a glowing nugget on my calendar. In bad times, like the last years of my marriage, Patricia's and Celia's house keys on my ring were promised solace, a ready escape from the sadness and the anger in my own home.

I still have Celia's key, but the door it opens is four hundred miles away. I need a more proximate haven. My thoughts turn to the low-slung über-modern house next door, occupied, according to my surreptitious surveillance, by a lesbian couple around my age. The women seem to have a vibrant social life—people always coming and going, laughter ringing through their walls.

Befitting our demographic, I handwrite them an actual note on actual paper and drop it into their actual mailbox.

Dear Ladies,

    This is your lonely lesbian neighbor. If you have any mercy in your souls, please accept my invitation to brunch, drinks, dinner, a hike, or all of the above, preferably at your earliest convenience.

A few hours later, my phone rings, a rare sound. "This is Donna. From next door." She laughs. "You've got our attention. Want to come over and have a drink with Nichole and me?"

"I thought you'd never ask," I say. "When's good?"

"You don't strike me as the patient type," Donna says. "How about now?"

When I get to the bottom of the quaking metal ladder, I find Donna and Nichole waiting for me there. One of them extends her hand. "I'm Nichole," she says. Her hair is black and curly, with white sprinkles. Her face is smooth and pretty and kind.

Donna is taller, also beautiful, with straight blond shoulder-length hair. "Help us out, Meredith," she says, grinning. "Nic and I have a bet going. She says there's no way you can actually be living at Karen's with that construction going on. But I've seen you in your dresses and heels in the morning, coming down that ladder like Tarzan. Who's right?"

"Me Tarzan," I say. "I'm cat-sitting for Karen for the next few weeks."

"Unbelievable," Nic says. They usher me through their front door and into their robin's-egg-blue, art-filled, light-filled living room. Two hours later I'm curled up on their pale yellow couch, shoes off, ginger margarita in hand. On the glass coffee table between us is a near-empty bowl of homemade guacamole, a crumple of cocktail napkins, a cheese board dotted with crumbles of Gouda and blue. Outside the room's floor-to-ceiling windows, the San Fernando Valley is a smoggy purple carpet unrolled to the Santa Monica Mountains.

And right next to me are two women I didn't know this morning, asking exactly the right questions with exactly the right looks on their faces, nodding at exactly the right times. Against all odds, we're laughing. And I'm feeling incredibly at home.

Nichole excuses herself to whip up a fresh pitcher of margaritas, pour another bag of chips. "It's horribly short notice," Donna says. "But we have a little shindig every year on the Fourth. Any chance you could join us?"

DESPITE, OR MAYBE BECAUSE OF, my attachment to my friendships, I've always done a crap job of diversifying them. Most women I know are pretty attached to monogamy with their sexual partners and pretty relaxed about sharing their friends. Having received my free-love diploma in the freewheeling 1960s, I've always been the opposite. My wife wasn't sold on lifelong monogamy, either; it made us both feel better to leave that door open, whether we chose to walk through it or not. (Not.)

Monogamous friendship has been a trickier balancing act, requiring me to convince my friends to obey my neediness-based rules and regs: a set schedule of frequent dates, the cohosting of extravagant birthday celebrations (hers, mine), shared vacations, round-the-clock availability, and full disclosure. By which I mean Full. Disclosure.

On both of our parts.

Of everything.

All the time.

Obviously, my approach to friendship has got to go. I have exactly three friends in Los Angeles, and I suspect that despite my arrival, Charlotte, Donna, and Nichole might want to keep the friends they already have.

A friend a day will keep the ER away. I need to increase my pool of friends; divide my needs by the largest possible number—in other words, change my definition of friendship from "You be everything I need you to be" to "I love you and you and you for who you are."

With or without my ridiculous rulebook, I find it daunting to reach out to strangers. Being happily married, being the primary source of my wife's happiness made me feel successful, confident, grounded. Having then become the source of her misery and my own, without understanding how that happened or why, makes me doubt that I'll ever feel that good about myself or anyone else or life again.

"The ultimate touchstone of friendship is . . . witness," I read in David Whyte's 2015 *Consolations*, "the privilege of having been seen by someone and the equal privilege of being granted the sight of the essence of another."

I know what I need to do if I'm going to see and be seen by new friends, and I don't want to do it. I need to learn to love and soothe myself, blah blah blah, instead of counting on others to do that for me. I need to seek less relief from others, blah blah, and learn to resolve my own anxieties by myself.

Until now I've managed to avoid being responsible for my own happiness, primarily by being coupled. At sixteen, I ran away from home to live with David. At twenty, I ran away from David to live with John. I was married to the father of my sons for twelve years, followed by twelve years of wimmyn-loving with my first girlfriend, Jane. I thought I'd kicked the marriage habit when Jane and I ended. But then a friend introduced me to my wife.

Since age fifteen I've been burying my emptiness under the rock of marriage. That rock has rolled. There's no one left to fill that space. My own efforts will have to do.

As depicted on social media, I've made a carefree career move to an exciting new city where I'm seeing new sights, taking sun-saturated pix, and having a swell time. The pretty illusion offers a vision of my future happiness, but I'd rather have a real life. So I swallow my pride and send a mass e-mail to my bicoastal writer friends who bounce between New York, where they write their novels and screenplays, and Hollywood, where they go to try to sell them.

"Dear people," I write. "I'm in desperate need of friends—IRL, not virtual—who live in L.A. I'm writing to ask you to introduce me to anyone you think I might like."

In for a dime, in for a dollar. I post a version of this message on Facebook and Twitter. Within hours, names start rolling in. And so my life as a friendship speed dater begins.

Michelle, an L.A. novelist friend of a New York novelist friend, asks me to meet her at a happy hour spot near UCLA at six-thirty on Tuesday night. I get out of work in Hollywood at five-thirty and start driving the eighteen miles. It takes two hours.

Still, I arrive before Michelle does. And then she's striding to-ward me, red hair flying, blue eyes flashing, wide mouth curved into a welcoming smile. By the time we've emptied our first pitcher of jalapeño margaritas, we've poured our hearts out to each other.

"Shit! It's ten o'clock." Michelle signals the waiter for our check. "This has been great, dollface, but I gotta go."

"Same time next week?" my inner needy child blurts.

"Love to," Michelle says, sounding like she means it. "But it ain't gonna happen. I live in the O.C."

She catches my blank gaze. "Orange County. It's an hour away"—she curves her fingers into air quotes—"without traffic. But we'll e-mail and text. And I come to L.A. a lot for book stuff. We'll see each other then."

Michelle grabs her purse and jumps to her feet.

"Or you can come down any weekend," she adds. "Unless you have something better to do than watch me yell at my husband and my kid and muck out my horse's stall."

"You have a *horse*? I *love* to ride! I had a horse when I was a hippie in Taos." I regret my blathering instantly. Michelle is in her mid-forties. Her *parents* were probably hippies.

"All my L.A. friends say they'll come see me. They never do," Michelle says matter-of-factly. I follow her flying mane through the restaurant doors. "Sincere promises, no follow-through. It's an L.A. thing."

She turns to hug me. "Let's talk soon." She laughs. "Saying 'Let's talk soon' instead of making a plan? That's an L.A. thing, too." And she's off.

It's not Michelle's job to fill your empty calendar, I tell myself, slogging east on Santa Monica Boulevard, only slightly less congested at ten p.m. than it was when I was slogging west at six. Even without a plan to see Michelle again—hello, demon disappointment—our encounter leaves me feeling less alone.

ENCOURAGED, I continue making my sales calls. Over the next month I have a "date" with a different writer at a bar or coffee shop or hiking trail, two or three times a week.

L.A. seems to be brimming with bright, creative people, drawn here, no doubt, by "the biz." Bonus factor: half a million of my fellow Angelenos are Jews—a bigger population of Chosen People than any other American city except my hometown, New York. Once again I'm living in a city whose worst pastrami sandwich is better than the best pastrami sandwich pretty much anywhere else. Once again I'm surrounded by loud, aggressive, impatient, intrusive, arrogant, sarcastic, nosy, hilarious, uninhibited, curly-haired people—my people. I figure that ups my odds of understanding and being understood by the strangers I'm hoping to turn into friends.

Sure enough, I'm amazed by the instant intimacy I share with the women I meet on my friendship dates, the quick bonds we build. Most of them are keepers: smart, funny, stylish, open, interesting, kind. Maybe it's the Jew factor, the DNA-level recognition that we were once cousins in Kiev. Or maybe my usual defenses, judgments, and desperation have fallen through the cracks in my broken-open heart.

A COUPLE OF MONTHS IN, I get a Facebook message from Lorelei Steele. I recognize the name. I used to read about Lorelei in the gossip column when the *San Francisco Chronicle* was my newspaper, and she was an elderly (which now means "ten years older than I am") San Francisco socialite.

Lorelei messages that she's a longtime fan of my writing. She, too, relocated to L.A., a couple of years ago. She invites me to lunch at her place in Beverly Hills. Yes is what I say to every invitation, these days, and yes is what I say to her.

Even taking into account Lorelei's social status, I'm stunned, pulling into her circular gravel driveway and parking in front of the three-car garage. The house is long and low, with tall white columns flanking massive, intricately carved wooden front doors. Before I can knock, the doors glide open, dwarfing the small woman who stands in the archway, her uniform stiff and white.

"I'm Carmen. Ms. Steele is waiting for you," she greets me. I follow her through rooms of floor-to-ceiling antique mirrors, burgundy velvet drapes with braided gold tiebacks, plump snow-white sofas and easy chairs scattered with pillows in contrasting floral patterns and skins. Ornate chandeliers hang from the ceilings; thick wool rugs pad the gleaming wide-boarded floors. One room is painted blood red; the next, pale yellow; the next, Wedgwood blue. All these colors and patterns in one house should be nauseating. Somehow they're magnificent instead.

Carmen leads me through Lorelei's boudoir, a fluffy palace of fainting couches and hat stands dripping with veils and gauze and life-sized oil portraits in baroque gold frames. The king-sized bed is an island of down duvets and silk-covered pillows and glossy percale shams, the feathered inner sanctum of a queen. Carmen opens a narrow French door and we're outside, breathing rose-scented air.

"There you are." Lorelei waves gaily from her seat at a small round table in the center of a lush garden in full, riotous bloom. In her straw hat, platinum pageboy, and floral linen dress, Lorelei herself is a bouquet. Even my untrained eye can see that her nips and tucks, her Bettie Page hairdo, and her makeup have been executed by the best in the biz.

Lorelei stands and pulls me into her distinctly maternal embrace. How sweet it is to be hugged by someone who's older than I am.

"Carmen, we'll have our lunch now, please."

"Yes, Miss Lorelei." Carmen ducks her head and disappears.

"Sit, darling," Lorelei instructs me. The table is covered with a charming mélange of multi-patterned place mats and mismatched floral china teacups and saucers and plates. In the near distance, a canopied white daybed scattered with cabbage rose pillows invites a tryst or a nap or, I fantasize, a day of writing, its linen curtains drawn against the desert sun.

"Tell me everything," Lorelei says, as if this were our hundredth lunch, not our first. So I do.

Lorelei and I are leaning into each other, our faces inches apart, when Carmen returns with a rolling glass cart laden with mango chicken salad and sourdough rolls and butter balls and tall glasses of mint iced tea.

"The same thing happened to me," Lorelei is saying. "Except I was *seventy* when my third husband broke my heart. He was the only one I truly loved. I'd been in San Francisco my whole adult life. I was the laughingstock of the town.

"I had friends on the board of every hospital and charity, a wardrobe full of designer clothes, a stunning home overlooking the Bay. I let go of all of it. I got in my car and I told my driver, 'Take me to Los Angeles.' I never looked back, and I've never regretted it."

Lorelei reaches over the plate of pastel petits fours embellished with fondant roses and takes my big hands in her velvety little paws. Her grip is bony but firm. "You're young and smart and pretty," she says. "You've got your whole life ahead of you. Don't worry, darling. You'll be fine."

I can't help but laugh. "Smart, yes," I say. "For all the good it did me. But young and pretty . . ."

Lorelei frowns. "You might never be happy again exactly as you were. But you *will* know joy again. Maybe in ways you can't even imagine now. Trust me. You'll see."

Two hours later Lorelei and I are standing in her foyer, a huge gold-plated statue of Buddha looming over us as we hug goodbye. "Come back soon," she says. "Come write in the garden anytime." I drive east from Beverly Hills feeling as if I just had a rose-scented dream. Me, the lifelong activist, lunching with a socialite? Who'da thunk it? This new life could hardly be more different from the old.

AFTER MY KIDS' FATHER and I divorced in 1984, I moved us to North Oakland because I could (and did) buy a cottage there for $180,000, and because I wanted our family to be part of the solution, not part of the problem. To me, this meant giving my kids a less segregated, less homogeneous, more socially engaged childhood than the one I'd had. I didn't want token diversity for my kids; I wanted theirs to be the generation that began to Eracism.

So my sons grew up riding their bikes behind mine like duck-lings to San Francisco Mime Troupe agitprop plays at UC Berke-ley, and taking BART with me to demonstrations for workers' rights, women's rights, gay rights, and immigrants' rights, and against war and inequity and police brutality. The friends they made in their public schools—and their friends' moms and dads, who became my parenting village and my close companions—were African American, Latino, Asian, biracial, and white, with all kinds of family structures and jobs and languages and reli-gions and cuisines and takes on life. This wasn't some liberal ex-periment, a white-guilt masquerade ball, a sacrifice. This was life as we knew it, and it was good and rich and real.

Then crack cocaine came to Oakland, and blood ran in the streets. Suddenly the darkness was pelted by gunfire; overhead, helicopters chopped the days into bits. One night the OPD chased a fleeing suspect in a Mazda RX7 through our front gate and across our front lawn; luckily, the car came to a stop two inches from our front door. One afternoon a man and a woman, argu-ing as they walked by our house, started screaming and hitting each other until the woman fell to the ground and fractured her skull on the cement. As the population of crack addicts in our neighborhood multiplied, kids my sons' ages started standing guard on street corners, lookouts for the dealers who lured them out of school with crisp fifty-dollar bills.

In the fall of 2011, Occupy Wall Street sprang to life across the country, and after two years of marital war my wife and I sprang into Occupy Oakland together. Our private hostilities fell away and we fell into the movement together as comrades, lifted up out of our petty bickering, absorbed by the joyful, determined spirit of the most exciting social change crusade either of us had ever joined.

For forty-five years I'd been an activist in various movements, most of them predominantly white and middle-class despite our best, most inclusive intentions. I was stunned by Occupy's popularity and diversity, especially given its simple, radical premise: that America's wealth should serve the vast majority, not just the tiny elite.

During that brief détente, my wife and I began many of our days at the ragtag Occupy encampment in downtown Oakland, shoulder to shoulder, serving donated bagels and coffee, tidying the Occupy library, picking up trash. When demonstrations were announced on Twitter or the local Pacifica radio station, we'd race downtown to fall into line with a throng of thousands, marching up Telegraph Avenue to join the students at Occupy UC Berkeley, or through residential Oaktown neighborhoods, where people poured out of decrepit apartment buildings and into our parade. On the day of the Oakland general strike, my wife and I marched with 25,000 to 100,000 (media/police count versus Occupy's) union members and anarchists and homeless people and reactivated sixties people and schoolteachers to the Port of Oakland and we shut it down.

In cities and towns across the country, police were raiding and dismantling Occupy encampments, tossing sleeping bags and tents and makeshift outdoor furniture and books. When Occupy Oakland fell, the renewed love between my wife and me died with it. Five months later I was on the road to L.A., and all I wanted was beauty and quiet and ease.

How strange that L.A., of all places, is giving me those things.

Even "with traffic," in twenty minutes I can hike to a hawk's-eye view of the Pacific. Graffiti artists turn freeway underpasses into Kahlo-esque murals.

Best of all, contrary to popular belief, L.A. is proving to be a great place to make friends. The classic stereotypes—angry Angelenos stranded on gridlocked freeways; wasteland miles of strip-mall sprawl; leggy blondes teetering out of auditions in stilettos; muscle-bound surfer boys living only to paddle out and rip back in—are all true. But the opposite also seems to be true. For smart, caring, authentic Angelenos like Donna and Nichole, and Charlotte, and yes, my new socialite friend Lorelei, making connections with kindred spirits is the stuff of social survival.

A NOVELIST NAMED HANNAH invites me to dinner at her house in Santa Monica. I'm not the #rookiemove driver I used to be. I tell her that I commute to the Westside on weekends only, and only during daylight hours. Hannah laughs, commenting, "You learn fast," and we make a date to meet for a hike on Saturday morning at a trailhead near Malibu.

Hannah and I were introduced via e-mail by Todd, our mutual book editor. "You'll love Hannah," Todd told me. "She's brilliant. Jewish. Your age. Real."

"Real" is evident in the car Hannah emerges from, and the dog she emerges with. Although she created a prime-time TV series and worked in "the biz" for decades, she's a novelist now. She drives an unstylish Chrysler SUV. Her dog is a mutt, not a designer "oodle." And somehow she's managed to make it in this town with a double-digit-sized body, zero makeup, messy (but not stylist-tousled) hair, in workout gear from REI instead of regulation Lululemon.

"Thanks for coming to the Westside," Hannah says. She taps the head of her white-muzzled dog. "This is Mabel. She's our age in dog years."

I bend to pet Mabel, hoping our geriatric hike won't be slowed down too much by Hannah's geriatric dog.

I follow Hannah up the steep, winding trail. As we walk and talk, fanned by the occasional cool ocean breeze, Hannah tells me about her abusive first marriage, which coincided with the years she spent in an industry she despised.

"I had to pretend to care about things that didn't matter to me at all," she says. "When I turned sixty I quit so I could pay attention to the things that do." She talks about her adored husband and two grown children with passionate affection, the same way she talks about the characters in her new novel.

"Todd said you moved here because your life fell apart," Hannah says, squinting into the too-bright light glinting off the too-blue ocean below. The trail narrows suddenly, and the mountain falls away on both sides. Hannah, her dog, and I are balanced on a precipice overlooking the endless ocean, the mansions of Malibu, the Ferris wheel revolving lazily on Santa Monica Pier. Even Mabel seems intimidated, curling herself around Hannah's scuffed, dusty boots. "Do you feel like telling me what happened?" Hannah asks.

Starting over with all new people gives me the option of crafting myself as a new character in a new story, of trying on a new persona every night of the week if I want to, just to see what fits. Lately when I'm asked a standard-life question, I pause before I spit out my old answer. If no one in L.A. knows that my decor style runs to Craftsman cottages and overstuffed couches, could I now be a person who favors midcentury-modern houses and chrome-and-leather chairs? My old friends knew better than to try to drag me to gray, frigid Northern California beaches, but maybe with my new friends I'll be a beach person who frolics in the warm Southern California waves. Why would I say that my favorite flavor of cupcake is chocolate, when the pink box in the office kitchen offers maple-bacon and salted caramel and lavender-thyme?

I give Hannah the abbreviated version, including the nightmares I've been having nearly every night since I left Oakland. "I've been a glass-half-empty person all my life. I'm trying to change that," I tell her. "But it seems like all the grief I swallow during the day, trying to focus on happier things, comes out when I sleep at night."

Hannah looks thoughtful. "You're trying to recover from PTSD *and* change your perspective on life," she says. "That's a lot to do at once. You have to trust that it's all proceeding at a pace your psyche can handle."

"I'm not sure I have enough time left to change. I'm a pretty fucked-up person."

Hannah stops, turns, peers at me through smudged aviator shades. "What's so bad about you?" she asks.

The question stops me for a moment. And then I tell her what I've been told; what, in the absence of a better story, I've come to believe. "I do what I want to do, without considering other people. I get what I want at other people's expense."

"Hmmm." Hannah gazes at me with brown eyes that look

familiar somehow. "I get that you're a person who goes for what she wants," she says slowly. "But I also get that you're really open to what other people say."

Hannah shakes out a pair of retractable walking sticks and we start back down the mountain. Her sticks click against the rocky trail in syncopated time.

"Maybe you've been hanging around with the wrong people," she says. "Maybe you just need to be with people who know how to say what they want."

A band of whooping teenage boys comes thundering down the trail from behind us. Hannah presses herself against the hillside, pulling Mabel close.

"When we were making plans for today," Hannah says, "you said you wanted to spend the whole day hiking. I said I only had two hours. You accepted that. You made it really easy for me to say no."

That's because I'm on my best behavior, I tell Hannah silently, because I'm desperate for you to like me. Wait till you get to know me. You'll see what's wrong with me.

SEVEN

After three months, although the L.A. body is not yet mine, the L.A. workout way is becoming my way. On Workout Wednesdays, lately, I've been forcing myself to focus on my own body instead of the bodies and outfits around me, which has transformed those sessions from ego-bashings to a net boost. There's more push in my push-ups, and each week I continue running a bit farther before devolving into a walk. I do fewer "wimp modifications," as Joanne calls them, and more of the full-on exercises the others do. At that blessed moment each week when Joanne packs up her TRX straps and the Bellas jostle into line for the shower, I notice an uptick in my energy and my mood.

In my Bellissima employee handbook, I uncover benefits yet unmentioned. For the first time in decades, I have dental insurance, plus coverage most of my coworkers won't be taking advantage of anytime soon: free eye exams and a free pair of glasses each year. If I should give birth to or coparent a baby, I'll get six months' paid leave. Also included at no cost to me: a membership to Silverado Gym.

Office buzz describes Silverado's Hollywood gym as *Boogie Nights* on steroids, the workout venue of choice for gay men who work the suburban stage sets of the San Fernando Valley, where 90 percent of American porn was produced before our laptops started streaming our own.

On the off chance that every study ever conducted and my own experience are correct, and exercise improves mental health, I sign up for a series of classes at Silverado: Bionic Booty on Saturday mornings, BodyPump and Power Abs after work. Seeing those entries on my iCal makes me appear to be having a life.

Saturday morning finds me in a humid, slightly stinky studio, awaiting my first class. Most of my fellow students are hot young gay men. The other two women in the room are in possession of the L.A. body. Then there's me.

"Morning, everyone! I'm Geoffrey. G-E-O-F-F-R-E-Y. I'll be your Bionic Booty instructor today." A human Hummer with visible nipple piercings bounces in place on bubblegum-pink Nikes.

Geoffrey squints across the dimly lit workout studio at the clock on the back wall. "We have four minutes till class starts. So! Who's got gossip? Anyone book anything this week? Got gay-married? Got an STD?"

None of his students respond. They're all squatting on their exercise mats, bent over smartphones, frantically texting as the moment of disconnect looms.

Geoffrey stretches his massive muscled arms above his head. "C'mon, people," he exhorts us. "Anyone got industry dirt? Celeb sightings? Rumors? Good news to share?"

If there are any celebs in the room, I wouldn't know it. Gay male porn happens to be the only variety that does nothing for me. You could knock me over the head with Jeff Stryker's mythic member and I wouldn't know whose it was, or maybe even what it was.

Geoffrey trains his gaze on the muscleman in the front row.

"Edward?" he says enticingly.

"I got nothing," Edward says.

Geoffrey sighs theatrically. "I get it. You're keeping your news to yourself in case someone in here tries to steal your booking. Or your date. I don't blame you. This is a tough town."

A ripple of agreement flutters through the room.

"This is a tough town," Geoffrey repeats. He turns the twin bowling balls of his ass to us and punches a button. "I Will Survive" blasts into the room. Geoffrey drops to his back on a mat, links his fingers behind his shaved head, and starts pumping out bicycle crunches. "At first I was afraid, I was petrified . . ." he sings along.

I watch myself in the floor-to-ceiling mirror, doing my own version of Geoffrey's moves. My body doesn't have his defined, bulging muscles. My twists are impeded by a ridge of belly fat and a lifetime of lazy workouts. My pace is slower, slightly behind the beat.

But I see something new on my face, besides sweat. Determination. I like the look of it. If my body can get stronger, maybe my heart can, too.

"I will survive!" Geoffrey shouts. His thighs are pistons in the air.

Who knows? Maybe I will, too.

The next song blasts from the speakers. "It's raining men, hallelujah," Geoffrey shouts.

When the music stops, the men around me start toweling off their Botoxed faces, putting away their weights and mats and resistance bands, making Grindr dates on their phones. I imagine them enjoying the rest of their sunny Saturday: brunching, shopping, bionic booty calling.

"Good job, everyone," Geoffrey says. "Give yourselves a hand." My classmates ignore him, rushing off to their mani-pedis and fresh-pressed juiceries and porn shoots. I muster a smile. Geoffrey smiles back at me. The two of us give ourselves a hand.

ON MY WAY BACK to Karen's, I call Joanne and sign up for personal training sessions, every Thursday at 7:30 a.m. Each session will cost eighty dollars—less, Joanne tells me, if she pairs me with another client. "You're a social person. You'll like that better than going solo anyway. And plus"—she laughs—"you're cheap."

I don't know how Joanne intuited these things about me and I don't care. From now on, every Thursday morning—without coercing any of my brand-new friends into seeing me regularly, and at a third the price of a shrink—I'll have an hour with someone who will eventually get to know me.

"Right on both counts," I tell Joanne. "Sure, double me up."

AT MY FIRST SESSION Joanne introduces my workout buddy as Mike. I recognize him as Jimbo, a lead character on one of my favorite HBO shows. "Oh my God," I blurt before my brain has time to stop my mouth, "I watch you every week. You're such a good actor!"

Joanne inserts her body between Mike and me, a tiny referee. "Sorry. Meredith's new in town," she tells him. "Still starstruck. She'll get over it."

Highly unlikely. Unlike the locals, who manifest a studied indifference to the celebs who walk and work out among us, I refuse to play it cool. This is my fallback life, goddammit. I'm going to cherish every cheap thrill I can get.

"No worries," Mike says to me over Joanne's head, which comes up to his nipple. "I appreciate your appreciation." A frisson of excitement runs through me. He's just like his character! Such a sweet guy. And he's my workout buddy!

Turns out, pain is a great equalizer. Once Mike and I are splayed side by side on our bellies, he on the hamstring machine and me on the butt-blaster, both of us grunting and cursing and slickening the black vinyl benches with sweat, he isn't Jimbo anymore, and I'm not a starstruck Hollywood rookie. We are both, as our trainer keeps reminding us, "Joanne's bitches."

Halfway through our session Joanne sends Mike out on a run around the block and positions me in the shoulder-lift machine. "So what's your story?" Joanne asks, head cocked, eyes locked on mine.

"What do you mean?" I say, shoving my arms out and over my head.

"Why'd you move to L.A.? And start a new job at an age when most people are retiring? And how come you're so sad?"

I drop the handles with a deafening clank. "You can talk and work out at the same time," Joanne says.

I'm in no position to turn down an interested listener. I give Joanne the brief version.

"Wow," she says.

Mike returns from his run, red-faced and dripping. "Wow, what?" he says.

"Meredith was just telling me why she just moved to L.A. She's been through a lot."

I'm half horrified, half delighted by Joanne's disclosures. I guess personal trainers aren't bound by confidentiality rules.

"I'm sorry." Mike reaches out and squeezes my arm.

"Okay, you two," Joanne says. "Follow me to the boys' room."

"We're working out in the *men's bathroom*?" I sputter.

Joanne laughs and leads us to the back of the gym, where the free weights and the boys are. Big boys. Boys with arms the size of Virginia hams and chests like refrigerators and waists like Golden Age starlets'. Joanne gives me a set of ten-pound hand weights. Mike gets thirties. The two of us stand facing the mirror, his young TV-star face and my geriatric face both so scrunched up with effort, they almost look alike.

I'm dying to ask Mike about his costars and the plot for the coming season. But despite Joanne's optimism, I can't lift weights and talk at the same time. While we do our rows and presses and bicep curls, I eavesdrop on the men around us instead.

"Three studios have Marvel products coming out soon. They've all been overdeveloped. I'm taking mine back to Universal."

"Dude. Where are my notes?"

"I know, I know. I was up all night. I promise I'll get them to you tomorrow."

"I'd do him in a heartbeat. Wouldn't you?"

"My contractor's smokin' hot, but the renovation is taking *for-fucking-ever.*"

"I hear he's up for something big."

"I hear he *is* something big."

Apparently Mike has been eavesdropping, too. "Men." He sighs.

"I HAVE A SURPRISE FOR YOU," Joanne says when I arrive for my second session. "I'm pairing you up with a lesbian. And she's single."

She grins at me, clearly pleased with herself. Trainer, therapist, *and* yenta. Not bad for sixty bucks a week. "Thanks. But I'm not—"

"*Shhh!*" Joanne waves to a shorthaired, stocky woman in track shorts and a Walk to End Breast Cancer T-shirt.

"Hey," the woman says, glancing at me, then at Joanne.

"Andrea, Meredith," Joanne says. "Meredith, Andrea. Okay, you two. Take a run around the block. Get to know each other."

As we set off Joanne yells after us, "Andrea! Meredith's a lazy-ass! Make her keep up."

Andrea and I jog toward Santa Monica Boulevard in silence. Even if I could talk and run at the same time, we wouldn't be conversing. Andrea looks angry, locked into herself.

"Andrea, sit-ups," Joanne barks as we run back into Silverado. "Meredith, come with me."

"So?" Joanne links her arm with mine, half dragging me to the butt-blaster. "What do you think?"

"Not my type," I say. "But thanks for trying."

Joanne stops fussing with the weight plates and looks across the gym at Andrea, who's doing crunches on a slant board. "There's a reason I put you two together," Joanne says quietly. "Andrea lost her wife, too."

"How long ago did they break up?"

"They didn't."

Joanne pauses for dramatic emphasis. "Oh," I say. "Cancer?"

Joanne shakes her head. "They were camping in Yosemite, celebrating their fifteenth anniversary. They went for a hike. Her wife slipped and fell off the side of the hill."

"Oh, God. Did she . . . ?"

Joanne nods. "The last thing Andrea saw was her wife's terrified face before she lost her grip. There was nothing she could do but watch her wife fall to her death."

"Oh my God," I say. "How is Andrea even walking and talking?"

"Same way you are."

"I'm going through a *breakup*. She watched her wife *die*."

"What happened to you is worse, in a way," Joanne says. "She lost her wife in an instant. You lost your wife over and over again. Every day. For years."

My stomach rumbles.

"You're *still* losing your wife," Joanne adds. "And you don't even know why."

I taste the hot sting of vomit in my throat.

"Are you okay?" Joanne asks. "You look kind of green."

I nod, then run to the bathroom, stand over the toilet, retching, thinking, I don't even know why.

MY LABOR DAY ANXIETY is starting to build when I get an e-mail from Carol, a member of Donna and Nichole's extended family of friends. Carol and I have gone to the movies and out for happy hour a few times, just the two of us. She's tall and stylish and smart, with a quirky sense of humor that matches mine.

Hi, Meredith! We have seats at the Bowl on Saturday to hear Ziggy Marley. If you don't have plans, like reggae music, and don't mind the last-minute invite, please come and join us as our guest.

I count to twenty, my hedge against appearing overeager, and write back telling Carol that the Hollywood Bowl is at the top of my to-see list. "What can I bring?" I ask.

"Just your beautiful self," she answers.

My heart soars. *Friends.*

At the designated meeting time I walk to Donna and Nichole's, carrying a tin of homemade pecan sandies, warm from my borrowed oven. I find the women packing picnic baskets and canvas totes and coolers into Carol's Audi.

"Naughty girl." Carol mock-scowls at the tin in my hands. "Which part of 'Don't bring anything' didn't you understand?"

Seventy-five minutes later, we've made it through the Saturday night logjam on the 101 to Hollywood, and the red-lights-for-miles crawl into the Bowl parking lot, and the loop-the-loop in the lot, looking for a spot that won't leave us trapped in a long line of cars when it's time to leave. Schlepping grocery bags and baskets and pulling a rolling cooler, we file into the Hollywood Bowl—the Hollywood Bowl!—bobbing along in a river of people carrying similar things. I follow my friends to our seats. Our seats are actually a box. In the second row. Twenty feet from the stage.

"Wow," I say. "You girls know how to live."

"What else is there?" Nichole says.

I shake off a wave of envy of Nichole and Donna's thirty-five-year, seemingly solid relationship, a wave of longing to be sharing this evening with my wife. I look around, taking it all in. The amphitheater is cut into the curve of the hill, ringed with rows of benches like a terraced vineyard. The rainbow-arched bandstand collides softly with the sky. I realize that some of my favorite TV shows and movies were shot here. *A Star Is Born*, the original 1937 version. *Beaches. Seinfeld. Californication.* My heart trills the way it does in these moments of recognition, falling a bit more in love with L.A.

"I'll be back," I say. I climb the wide stone steps past the front rows, where mostly white, middle-aged boxholders are pouring wine and setting out cheese platters. I pass the mixed crowd of the middle ground, where partyers are drinking Red Stripe beer. In the nosebleed seats, a younger, darker-skinned crowd in dreadlocks and crocheted Rastafarian caps are dancing to the piped-in reggae, passing spliffs, creating their own weather, a cloud of pot smoke hanging heavy in the hot night air.

From the uppermost ledge of the Bowl, I look down at the eating, drinking, smoking, swaying masses. Beyond the band shell, the parched Hollywood Hills squat on the horizon. As I watch, the sun sinks an inch. Maybe it's the contact high, but the last shafts of daylight seem to light up the Hollywood sign.

How did I get to be here, in this beautiful place with these beautiful people? My chest swells with a feeling I remember. Happiness. Freewheeling, free-floating joy.

If I can have one good moment, I tell myself, I can have two. If I can have two good moments, maybe I can build a pile of good moments, good hours, good days.

The warm-up band struts onto the stage. I give myself a home-work assignment for the evening. I won't go home till I've had at least one more good moment. As is true of the Rastas and wannabe-Rastas around me, the odds of that seem high.

"Where you been, M&M's?" Carol sings out to me.

"Checking out the lay of the land."

"Laid? You should get so lucky," Donna says, and we share a laugh.

Clearly this isn't my hosts' first Bowl rodeo; they're a well-oiled picnic machine. Carol shakes out a multicolored woven tablecloth, smooths it over the table, sets out blue paper plates and blue cloth napkins that pick up the color in the weave. Donna adds slender flutes and a tiny bud vase, inserts a perfect yellow rose. Nichole sets out a bowl of Mediterranean chicken with couscous. Carol opens a Tupperware container of Greek salad, her specialty.

Donna pops the cork on a bottle of Moët. The four of us let out a cheer.

"To music and friendship, the perfect concert." Nichole raises her flute. We toast one another, swaying to the reggae from the stage.

Hallelujah: Joy! I drink to it. I welcome it. I tell it to come on in.

"Thanks for inviting me," I say, spooning couscous, chicken, salad onto my plate.

"No thanks required," Donna says, half-full flute in hand. "You're part of the family now."

EIGHT

I t's finally over, Mer." My friend Emily weeps into the phone. "We're getting divorced."

"Oh, honey," I say. "I wish I was there to hold you right now."

"I wish that, too."

When Emily and I met at an artists' colony in 2006, it was loathing at first sight. That night, Emily told me later, she called her soon-to-be ex-husband, complaining about the boundaryless stalker (that would be me) who'd asked to use the bathtub in her room. That same night I called my wife, complaining about the arrogant snob who wouldn't let me borrow her tub. The next afternoon Emily and I shared a ride to town and actually spoke to each other and fell madly in friendship love.

The immediate intense intimacy between us outlived our residencies, as many colony friendships do not. Over the next decade there were rescue missions undertaken on a few days' notice, back when book advances supported impulsive air travel. There were late-night 911 calls when a publisher or a spouse or a therapist or a friend let one of us down, and shared vacations with our families, and hikes in the Northwest rain forest and in the Oakland hills.

Seven hundred fifty miles and fourteen years apart, we found our crises and triumphs eerily synchronistic. My menopausal breakdown, her perimenopausal paroxysm. The delights and stresses of renovating a hundred-year-old, three-story house—hers on a broad, leafy Olympia street, mine in the Oakland flats. Our trials and errors with the meds and the sexual side effects of the meds and the weight gain with the meds and the adjusting of the meds and the ambivalence about the meds: If antidepressants pull us two steps back from our suffering, we worried, do they also distance us from the emotions that make us who we are, the emotions that fuel our work? Are Wellbutrin and Zoloft the modern equivalent of our mothers' Miltown and Valium, keeping us well adjusted to people and institutions that should be adjusting to us?

As I struggled to salvage my marriage, Emily struggled to breathe life into hers. Each of us knew that the other one's marriage couldn't last, long before we could quite face that truth about our own.

"I'm coming to be with you," I say.

"Honey. You have a job. And you're broke." Emily blows her nose. "I'd buy you a ticket, but I'm broke, too."

"I'll use miles," I say. "I'll come for a long weekend." Over Emily's protests, I book a ticket and go.

"SO MUCH BETTER THAN FACETIME," Emily says, clinging to me.

"We need the bodies, you and me," I agree, kissing her face.

"While you're here," Emily says, driving, "I want us to make a place for me to write in my new place."

"Easy," I say.

"On no money."

"Who needs money?"

"I want to talk about everything," Emily says. "But not now."

"Who's asking questions?" I say. "Let's get to work."

ON THE LONG LIST of happinesses that being married brought me, nest-feathering was very near the top.

Nothing says "I'm one with you" like picking out a mattress together, or going cross-eyed holding paint chip after paint chip up to a kitchen wall. The domestic projects my wife and I did together—hunting down period fixtures for our Victorian bathroom, hanging found objects in our backyard trees, shopping for champagne flutes at the Crate & Barrel outlet store, all while holding hands—made my heart melty. Each jointly chosen plate and rug became the living embodiment of the "we," the "us," the "ours" that I thought would save me, and did save me, for a time.

At the Spokane Target, helping Emily fill a shopping cart with cheap unassembled bookshelves and curtain rods and picture frames, I'm surprised to feel that familiar happiness. As we drive to Emily's new apartment, decide where to put each new purchase and which problem each new item will solve, my chest swells with belongingness and love.

Emily parks in front of a beige-brick apartment building. Her face goes glum. "This is it," she says. "It's horrible."

What nice thing can I say about my friend's reduced circumstances, the price of her emancipation? Like mine, Emily's post-divorce dwelling is a steep comedown from her marital home. Like my wife and me, Emily and her husband had spent a decade restoring their three-story Victorian to its turn-of-the-century glory. As a heterosexual divorcée in 1983, I memorized the stats about men's versus women's post-divorce finances: ex-husbands get richer; ex-wives, poorer. According to recent reports, nothing much has changed: in the first year after divorce, the wife's standard of living drops more than 25 percent; the husband's may increase by as much as 10 percent. As my husband did when we split up, Emily's ex will go on living in the family home.

Emily and I spend the weekend rearranging furniture, creating a writing nook in her living room, hanging drapes, and assembling bookshelves, talking and laughing and eating and drinking. We cook dinner together at night and cuddle in Emily's new bed in the mornings, smoothing the edges of our bodies' jagged need for touch. Saying good-bye on Sunday night is wrenching, but our history reassures us that we'll always end up in the same room at the same time when we really need to be.

Maybe I don't need to give up *everything*, I think, greeted by no one at Bob Hope Airport at midnight, dragging my suitcase off the baggage carousel and out into the dark night, past the shuttered rental car kiosks, across a four-lane street to the cheapo airport parking lot, where my car is still another unlit quarter-mile walk away. I don't have a wife to pick me up at the airport, but I can still hold and be held, comfort and be comforted.

As much as I've ached to end the months of couch-surfing, I've dreaded the thought of making a home alone. But maybe if I can feel good feathering a nest for Emily, I can feel good—or at least, survive—feathering a nest for myself.

UNTIL I STARTED LOOKING for a place to rent, I'd managed to ignore the panicky headlines about Los Angeles' affordable-housing crisis. Looking for a place I can afford snaps me out of denial. The reality is not pretty.

The average price of a single-family home in Los Angeles is nearly $800,000, so the rental market is flooded with would-be buyers turned renters. Meanwhile, the number of rentals has been shrinking, thanks in part to landlords turning whole apartment buildings into hyper-profitable Airbnb "hotels." Google's new Westside campus set hordes of house-hunting employees loose on neighborhoods already stretched beyond capacity. East Coast transplants are arriving in droves, weary of climate-changed winters, drawn by the promise of jobs in "new TV." The average rent for a two-bedroom apartment in Los Angeles is $2,591—$500 more than the mortgage on my three-story house in Oakland, and $500 more than I can afford.

Celia comes down from San Francisco to help navigate the search. We check out a "cute, cozy Hollywood cottage" for $1,450—perfect if not for three little problems: no kitchen, no windows, and a homeless man camped in the doorway. A $1,300 "updated studio" in a gloomy Koreatown apartment building does have a kitchen and two grime-encrusted windows overlooking a strip mall, but no stove.

As I scour the listings on my phone, Celia drives us toward Mount Washington, an outlying neighborhood where hipsters have only just begun their rent-inflating influx. "It'll take you an hour to get to work from here," Celia says. She knows I had to move to L.A., and she knows I have to stay in L.A. at least until my financial picture improves, but she doesn't have to like it. This up-close-and-personal tour of L.A.'s housing crisis isn't helping.

I decide to look for a "share situation" in a safer, more central neighborhood. Craigslist sends us to a "suite" in the Silver Lake home of a self-described "old Hollywood queen."

"Steps need work," Celia says, the railing rattling in our grip. A deeply tanned, deeply wrinkled eightysomething man in a gold lamé bathrobe and gold slippers shows us to the "suite": a single large room adjoining his bedroom. "Only the best!" Queenie beams proudly at the splintery gold-painted wood floor, gold-painted walls, and gold-painted ceiling.

Celia and I retreat to her car. She turns on the AC and we sit silently staring out at the smoggy sky. "You could come home and live with me," she says. "I'll support both of us till you get a job."

"You know I have to do this." I glance down at the phone in my lap. "The next place looks much better."

Celia sighs and drives me there. And yes, the "Writer's Villa" is a gorgeous, sprawling, terraced, and turreted Spanish-style mansion built into a Los Feliz hillside. The Villa is listed as a "writer's community," common areas shared, rooms rented to working writers by the week, month, or year.

Ruth, a screenwriter and the resident "house mother," gives us a tour of the lush jungle gardens, quaint tiled bathrooms, luxurious kitchen, and spacious Mission-styled living room with leather couches, TV, sound system, printers, and built-in bookshelves overflowing with award statuettes and books. We follow her up a winding wrought-iron staircase to the room that was recently vacated, she tells us, by a writer who switched from *NCIS: Los Angeles* to *CSI: Las Vegas*. My excitement evaporates as I look around the small, dark, drably furnished $2,700-a-month room. The view of Griffith Park is stunning, but the small window is north-facing, passed over by the sun. "You get to share the up-stairs terrace," Ruth says. "And the people who live here are great. The dinner conversations alone are worth the rent."

I glance at Celia, who's staring at the twin bed. "I'll think about it and get back to you," I say. Celia nearly runs me over on our way down the stairs.

"I need a place of my own," I say as she and I are polishing off a plate of fish tacos at Ricky's, a local dive that Celia frequented during her L.A. years.

Celia glances at her phone. "My flight's in two hours," she says. She drives me back to Karen's house, hugs me good-bye across the front seat.

"It helped so much to have you with me," I say.

Through gritted teeth she says, "Remember, you can always come home."

"No, I can't," I say. "But thanks."

Two weeks later I find a listing for a 500-square-foot fur-nished cottage in Silver Lake, "the hippest neighborhood in America," the neighborhood Berkeley would be if only Berkeley more willingly embraced the passage of time.

I rush to meet Bob, the landlord, at the cottage. The tour doesn't take long. There's a decent-sized living room, a dining area, a funky but serviceable kitchen, a tiny bathroom, and a small, sunny bedroom with a peekaboo view, as Bob calls it, of the Silver Lake hills. Best of all, the cottage is secluded, enclosed by a tall fence lashed with grapevines, and the shady little patio is outfitted with a resin Adirondack chair, so I can write outside. On the downside, it's across a narrow alley from a 7-Eleven store, which will situate my head exactly twelve feet from a rooftop air compressor that sounds like ten jets taking off at the same time. Bargain-priced at $2,200 a month, the cottage is a fifteen-minute drive from my job.

"I'll take it," I say. And then I remember from thirty years ago, the last time I rented a place, the way this game works. This isn't powerful me, choosing a house to rent. This is supplicant me, hoping to be chosen. "If you'll rent it to me," I add.

Bob sits down next to me on the beige Ikea couch, lays out copies of the rental agreement, and hands me a pen. As I'm printing my name next to my new address, my hand freezes.

I can't have a different address from my wife's.

Bob peers at me impatiently. I read him loud and clear. If I'm not ready to take the place, there are about a zillion people who are.

I sign the lease. I hand Bob a check for $4,400. He hands me the keys to my new home.

HAVING MY OWN PLACE to live is so much better than couch-surfing. Having a door to close. Plucking my underwear from drawers instead of suitcases. Leaving my shampoo and my tooth-paste in the bathroom instead of packing them in and out each time. Finding only my own clothes in the closet, my own food in the fridge.

My cottage is tiny, but in this climate, my space isn't. I buy a backpack chair and spend writing days at the Silver Lake reservoir park, cell phone in hand, laptop in lap, bare feet in moist, cool grass. At night I throw the cottage windows open, inhaling the twin Silver Lake scents of pot and skunk, dancing with myself to the music blasting from the indie rock club a block away.

Having my own place is also excruciating. My name on the mailbox, alone. My tea mug in the sink, alone. Nothing changes in the cottage unless I change it. If I forget to turn the TV off at night, it's still on when I wake up in the morning. No one makes the bed, helps use up the half-and-half before it sours, hangs her jeans over mine on the hook. If I want to put up curtains, replace the coffee table, buy firewood although the local weather calls for air-conditioning, that's up to me and me alone.

There's a question I ask myself at times like this, when my "acting as if" needs a boost. What would a normal person do when she moves into a new apartment?

She'd throw a housewarming party, that's what.

I can't throw a party. Parties are what my wife and I do together. But if I don't throw parties without my wife, I'll never throw a party again.

I call my new friend Hannah, who gives great dinners at her Santa Monica house. "I want to have a housewarming party," I tell her. "I was wondering—"

"Great idea," she says. "How can I help?"

HANNAH ARRIVES TWO HOURS BEFORE the guests, toting Whole Foods bags fragrant with the chickens and garlic potatoes she roasted and the bruschetta ingredients she prepped, and an extravagant bouquet of white lilies in a vintage glass vase. "Welcome home." She hands me the flowers and unpacks the trays, platters, and flutes she brought from home.

People come. Charlotte and her new boyfriend, Brian, and Donna and Nichole and their friends David and George. Michelle, my redheaded happy hour date, can't make it up from Orange County, so she sends two writer friends she says I need to know—Darcy, who lives up the street, and Molly, who drives all the way from the Westside.

My next-door neighbor Geneen, who restores vintage clothing. Rodolfo, the shucker from the oyster bar across the street, where I eat or drink a few times a week, just to hear him greet me by name.

Hannah's friends come, too. Our editor, Todd. A novelist who used to write for *Seinfeld*. A humor writer who, it turns out, wrote the *Sex and the City* episode in which Aidan leaves Carrie for cheating on him with Mister Big.

Music plays on borrowed speakers. People talk and laugh, eat and drink. Hannah helps me keep the wineglasses and platters filled and the dirty plates cleared. Everyone seems happy to be here and reluctant to leave.

Hannah insists on helping me clean up. It's near midnight when she packs her platters and glasses and brushes off my thanks and drives back across town.

Now is when my wife and I hug and high-five each other: another fabulous party thrown, another set of fabulous people introduced to each other, another abundance of delicious food served, more proof that we're so much bigger and better as a couple than either of us would be alone.

That was then. Now is when my empty house rings with silence. Now is when I find out what I can do and who I can be, alone.

Housewarming party, not pity party, I scold myself. I didn't throw it alone. I threw it with Hannah, my new friend.

I dry my landlord's pots and pans and put them where I want them to go, not necessarily where he left them, and mop the kitchen floor at one in the morning, grateful that I can bang around without waking the person whose couch I'm borrowing. My grief fights it out with that fragile shadow dancer, hope.

I don't have nearly as much time left as I did the last time I started over, at age forty-five, when I made a home with my wife. Time doesn't care. Healing isn't a moment, an epiphany, a turning point without reversals or twists. It's a process, and it's not up to me how long it takes or how it feels along the way.

It took a long time for all the good things I had—marriage, friends nearby, money—to fall into place. It's going to take a long time to get over losing them. Like it or not (not), this healing will be a wall I build solo, one brick laid down upon another brick and another.

In the interim I'm living my booby-prize life, wringing every drop of delight from the tiniest things. "Little victories," Kenny Loggins sang to me, "are all a heart needs." They're not all I need, but they help. Finding the perfect nightstand in my neighbor's bulky pickup pile. Treating myself to a po' boy at the oyster bar, to a day of window-shopping in Beverly Hills.

This wasn't the life I wanted. It isn't the life I want. But I'm here now, doing what I came to this tough, thrilling town to do.

Slowly, sometimes agonizingly, I'm restoring myself to financial, emotional, and spiritual health.

Like it or not (mostly not), I'm living my Plan B life here now.

I'm living here now.

I'm here now.

I'm here.

PART TWO

HALF-EMPTY

NINE

'm in a three o'clock meeting at Bellissima, brainstorming product names for the summer collection, when my phone vibrates in my pocket. It's my stepmother's ring.

My heart thuds. Lina e-mails; she never calls. I slip into the hallway to phone her back.

"Your father . . ." Lina can't talk because she's crying. Lina never cries. "He fell. He fell and I couldn't—"

"Lina," I interrupt her. "Is he alive?"

"Oh! Oh, yes. I'm sorry." She inhales an uneven breath. "But he is not good."

"Not good how?"

"He fainted. I could not wake him up." Lina's Swiss accent is thicker than usual, the way it gets when she's exhausted or upset.

I see my father on the floor in their San Francisco apartment, my stepmother trying to hoist him into bed.

It wouldn't be the first time. In the ten years since my father's diagnoses with Alzheimer's, diabetes, and heart disease, we've been lucky. For most of that decade he's been able to get himself to the bathroom, remember his children's names, and push a cart around Costco, his greatest pleasure once he could no longer manage a Giants game or Dollar Day at the track.

But for the past year he's been declining rapidly. Too proud to use a walker or a scooter, he gradually lost the ability to walk, discern day from night, or eat more than a few bites. The irony is painful: my chronically overweight father, who spent most of his life alternately researching new restaurants and new diet pills, had lost his interest in food.

"I called 911," Lina says. "They took him to the hospital. They say he's dehydrated. They're giving him fluids. Your brother and I are here with him now."

"Should I come?" I ask.

"When I was trying to get him off the floor," Lina chokes out, "he told me, 'I wish I could ride with you into the sunset.'"

"I'll be on the next flight," I say.

I call the airline and book a seat, then beckon Heather out of the meeting. How could she possibly understand what I'm about to tell her? Her parents are younger than I am. Her *grandparents* are all alive.

"My father's in the hospital in San Francisco." Saying the words makes my eyes burn. "I have to go."

"Of course you do. I'm so sorry," Heather says. "Anything we can do? Do you need a ride to LAX?"

I shake my head, hug her quickly, and head for the door. My flight takes off at 4:20. It's 3:05 now. It's going to be tight, but I have to make it. The next flight isn't until seven tonight.

I steer my car through the thickening rush-hour traffic,

willing the hands on my dashboard clock to stop moving, eyes glued to the rearview mirror in case I cross paths with a cop. I remember Isabel talking about a special airport valet service she uses when she's "really, *seriously*" late for a flight. Of *course* LAX offers an option for the rich. It must cost a fortune, but in this moment I'd mortgage my house to get to my dad.

Siri guides me to the airport valet. Before I've quite come to a stop, a young man in a black uniform runs up to my car, waves me into the passenger seat, and jumps behind the wheel. Two minutes later he drops me at the Southwest terminal, gives me a number to text my return flight number to, and drives away in my car.

I race up to the ticket counter, slap down my credit card. "The 4:20 to San Francisco," I say.

The ticket agent frowns, shakes her head. "They just locked the doors on that flight. I can get you onto the 7:04."

"That won't work," I open my mouth to say. Instead, I burst into tears. "My dad is in San Francisco, and he's dying," I choke out. "I have to get there *now*."

The agent bites her lip and starts typing furiously. "You're on the next United flight to SFO. It leaves in twenty minutes." She yanks a boarding pass out of the printer, hands it to me. "They're giving you the bereavement fare. Run."

"Thank you," I say to her and to God, and then I run. I run and run across the vast expanse of the LAX domestic terminal and I make it onto the plane just as the flight attendant is closing the door. I spend the hour-long flight leaning forward, as if that will get me there sooner.

Racing out of the cab and into the hospital lobby, punching

the elevator button again and again, I imagine my father on a gurney in one of these hallways, seeing what I'm seeing, smelling what I'm smelling, thinking what I'm thinking—but flat on his back, helpless, exposed. Like his father before him, my dad breathes fear the way calmer people breathe air. For most of his adult life, my father's time belonged to the corporations that paid our rent. Since he retired, he's been happily marooned on his gray leather recliner, the pleasure center from which he enjoys his baseball games and black-and-white movies, his privacy, his creature comforts, his time with his cherished wife.

The only thing that tortures my dad more than worrying about the people he loves is causing the people he loves to worry about him. My heart hurts, knowing that my father is living his worst nightmare in these last days—hours? minutes?—of his life.

On the sixth floor, a nurse points me to his room. I speed-walk down the hall, come to a stop in my dad's doorway. He's asleep in his hospital bed. He's alive.

Relief washes over me. But is this gray-faced, slack-jawed, disappearing man really my dad? Plastic bags hang off the sides of his bed. There's an oxygen tube in his nose. Monitors beep. I can feel him going. It will be better for him, worse for us, when he's gone.

My brother stands at the window, talking on his phone. My stepmother sits in an orange plastic chair next to my father's bed, staring red-eyed into space.

My dad's eyes flutter open, widen, and then narrow in on me. "Things must be worse than I thought," he says. "I see they brought in the big guns."

I choke back tears. My father doesn't know whether it's day or night or what country he lives in or which of his wives he's married to, but his sense of humor survives. All my life, he's been transfusing it to me. I won't always have my father, but I'll always have that.

I go to his bedside and hug him. "Hello, sweetheart," he says into my ear.

"Hey, Pops," I say into his. He pats my back nervously. I cling to him. How many more times will I hear him call me *sweetheart*, I wonder. We had so few hugs, our first sixty years. How many more do we get?

"How are you?" I ask.

"Too soon to tell. Ask me in ten years."

I shake my head at him, kiss Lina's cheek, hug my brother, and return to my father's bedside. "Really, Dad."

He meets my eyes. "The question is, how are *you*?"

For the past ten years, my dad has been on a mission, trying to make up for the previous fifty. He was a classic crappy 1950s middle-class father, Old Spice-scented, away on business trips a lot of the time, pretty much absent even when he was home. Like so many of his ilk, he was the reigning king of the castle, his lone minion my mom. He never knew the names of my friends or my schoolteachers. When he was in some Neiman Marcus somewhere, buying me a pair of fancy pajamas, he had to call my mother long-distance to ask for my size. But I adored my father and I absorbed his humor and his hungers, and somehow, despite his distance, despite his insistence that I mirror him instead of manning up and mirroring me, I knew that he adored me.

Until my adolescence broke up our mutual admiration society, my dad was my playmate and my role model. We stole weekend hours together, eating corned beef and coleslaw sandwiches at the Gaiety Deli, betting the long shots at Aqueduct, acting out the plays he wrote, recording them on the Sony reel-to-reel we drove downtown together to buy.

My father was a Madison Avenue ad man, Don Draper without the booze or the cigarettes or the style. His longing to be a real writer went underground in him and resurfaced in me. He asked me repeatedly what I wanted to be when I grew up. Unlike so many fathers of his time, he wouldn't take *wife* for an answer. The son of Holocaust-era Jews, my father fed me a steady stream of terrible, fear-driven advice. It was almost worth it for the one good bit he shared: "No matter how bad it is, a sense of humor will make it better."

My dad is asleep again. My brother taps me on the shoulder, beckons me out of the room.

"His doctor says it's time for hospice," my brother says.

"What does that mean?" I stall. I know exactly what hospice means. Patricia was in hospice care for a month, from the day she left the hospital until the day she died at home. She adored Lenny, her night-shift hospice nurse, because he read Kafka to her. One night, when Patricia was sleeping, Lenny told me that he'd never known anyone to live as long as Patricia was living on just a few ice chips a day. "Ice chips and Kafka," I added. "And Kafka," Lenny agreed.

"Maybe we can talk Lina into getting a full-time nurse," I tell my brother. "Or find a really good nursing home—"

"Mer," he says.

My stepmother, my brother, and I have been having this conversation off and on for the past year. As my father's symptoms have cascaded, his care has become impossible for my stepmother to handle, even with the help of a visiting nurse. Luckily and confusingly, my dad is still very much alive inside his failing body. In fact, his illness has made him humbler, more emotional, more lovable, and more loving, which makes knowing that we'll soon lose him extra hard.

I know there are countless daughters and sons and wives and husbands dealing with precisely this heartache. I know there's only one way out of life. Still, I can't let go of my conviction that there's some solution we could find (to mortality?) if only we were creative and persistent enough.

"Lina's against it," my brother says. "We have to convince her. If she brings him home again, this is just going to keep happening."

"You don't know that." Even to myself, I sound like a petulant child.

Lina takes my father home. My brother goes back to work. I fly back to L.A.

Three weeks later, I get a call from Lina, telling me to come quick—again. I race to the airport again, race to my father's hospital bed, and find my dad weak and disoriented but alive—again. I know this is the normal course of events. I know this is how it happens. I don't care. I don't want it to be happening, period. Checking in for my third flight back to L.A. in the past two months, I inquire about Southwest's bereavement fare. They don't offer one.

MY THERAPY SESSIONS with Olivia offer companionship and comfort and relief. But with my dad's clock ticking down and my system on 24/7 alert, I need a bit more ballast.

During the hard years with my wife, a Berkeley friend invited me to an Al-Anon meeting. "It'll help you keep the focus off what *she's* feeling and thinking and doing," she said, "and keep the focus on what you can do for yourself." I figured it couldn't hurt to stop analyzing every breath my wife took and start paying attention to breathing better myself. And it was free.

Much to my surprise, Al-Anon helped. A lot. So I started going to meetings every week. As weirdly ritualistic as the meetings were, as seemingly obvious as the program's guidelines for living were, hearing the sagas of other control freaks loosened my death grip on fate and opened a tiny keyhole inside me where faith began to grow.

"The God thing" that bugged my atheistic Berkeley brethren was actually a plus for me. I liked standing in a circle, holding hands with a roomful of strangers, saying the Serenity Prayer, invoking God's name. I liked the cleverness of the Al-Anon slogans, as good as any I'd heard (or written) during my marketing years.

"You didn't cause it, you can't control it, you can't cure it."

"FEAR = False Evidence Appearing Real."

"Don't judge your insides by other people's outsides."

"Progress, not perfection."

"Don't just do something. Stand there."

Reciting the Serenity Prayer—"God, grant me the serenity to accept the things I cannot change, the courage to change the things I can, and the wisdom to know the difference"—I'd close my eyes and try to imagine what on earth this strange sensation, serenity, might feel like.

On the Los Angeles Al-Anon website I find dozens of meetings, including one on Sunday mornings at an LGBTQ center a fifteen-minute walk from my house. The notion of praying for redemption on Sunday mornings with a bunch of gay people appeals to me, and so do the hilarious shares of the stand-up comics and sitcom writers in the room. My search for serenity is unlikely to be quick or easy. But at least I've found a welcoming place to look.

ON MY FIRST DAY BACK at Bellissima after my latest emergency trip to San Francisco, my coworkers welcome me with great kindness. They tell me they're sorry my dad is sick. They ask how he's doing. They ask how I'm doing.

I've been at Bellissima for eight months now, and until I ran out of the office crying on two separate occasions three weeks apart, no one besides Charlotte had asked me a single question about myself.

I know it's unfair to compare my coworkers' level of interest in me to my interest in them (and everyone else on earth). I'm blessed and cursed with a journalist's nosy nose; I come from a long line of buttinskis. But I've given my coworkers so much to wonder about. Why was a sixty-year-old woman available to move to L.A. on a moment's notice? Why did she arrive wearing a wedding ring, which was soon replaced by a hugely bandaged finger, and then by a stitched scar? Is she gay, straight, bi? Single, married, dating, divorced? Did she find a place to live in this wildly expensive city? Does she have friends or family here?

For a while I attributed my colleagues' lack of interest to the kind of polite restraint that's practiced by alien species (humans who are not New York Jews). Then I thought they were being respectful, waiting for me to initiate exchanges more personal than those revolving around their Paleo diets and makeup tips. But each attempt at clue-dropping left me standing in the empty lunchroom with a frozen smile on my face.

It took me a while, but I got it. My personal life is of no interest to my coworkers because my age makes me irrelevant to them. Just as my hippie comrades and I vowed never to trust anyone over thirty when we were their age, they have no reason to want me following them around. Their Facebook shenanigans—their club-hopping and Urban Outfitters shopping expeditions; their Tinder swiping and holiday pilgrimages to their parents' houses—will never include me. My divorce and my bulk-pickup-day-decorating and my sidelined writing career will never include, nor be a subject of conversation with, them.

The fact that I'm "young at heart," "young-looking for my age"? Irrelevant. My eagerness to plug into "youth culture" by learning my coworkers' tastes in music, clothes, diets, boyfriends? Irrelevant. Possibly also annoying.

On the other hand, the feminist complaint about the invisibility of older women—something I couldn't imagine ever applying to me? Highly relevant. Invisible, c'est moi. For thirty-two hours a week on the job, and 24/7 everywhere else.

The insult has its benefits. I don't have to make up stories about what I did over the weekend or whom I did it with. I don't have to change pronouns to ward off homophobia or change details to protect the innocent. On weekday mornings when I wake up crying, I can spackle my face with makeup and slap on a smile, knowing that no Bella will ask the kind of questions or give me the kind of sympathetic glance that might crack my façade.

Better late than never, I'm developing a social skill I've never wanted before: the ability to keep my feelings to myself. After a lifetime of believing that anything less than full disclosure equals withholding and discretion equals deceit, I'm seeing the upside of the boundaries I scorned. My work life gives me a break from my broken personal life. My competent work persona gives me a break from my broken self. Spending my workdays "acting as if" isn't just faking it. Mimicking a person who's capable of functioning is actually making me functional.

Huh.

FOR ONE HOUR each workweek, Workout Wednesday levels the playing field. If I can manage to keep up with the other Bellas, our shared sweaty suffering transcends the generation gap.

And so I try. Hard. I jog around the city block with the others when I'd *so* prefer to walk. I do twenty-five push-ups when I'm ready to quit at five. I do the goddamn burpees and the dead bugs and the rock climbers. I squat, I crunch, I lunge. I never miss a private training session with Joanne and I take classes at Silverado four nights a week and I see my body changing and I decide that I'm going to win the next Fat Contest at work, two months from now.

I join my young colleagues on the Paleo diet. In violation of my father's training and my entire Jewish lineage, I abandon the theory of preventative eating (in case the Cossacks come) and start eating for fuel, not pleasure. One hard-boiled egg and one slice of Canadian bacon for breakfast. A tiny mound of undressed chicken-kale salad for lunch. A huge mound of steamed vegetables for dinner. Two French fries instead of two pounds of French fries at happy hour with Charlotte. One bite of cake at the

Capricorn birthday party at work. One cocktail, not four, at Donna and Nichole's.

I like dieting. I like the rules, the restrictions, the structure. I like not having to think about what to eat. I like the bright line between "good" behavior and "bad." The craving for alcohol's edge-blurring never fades, but the cravings for fat and sugar recede. I decide to eat half as much and have a martini when I want one, which is every night. Thus I create my own sustainable diet.

On Weigh-In Wednesday Joanne sets up shop in the office bathroom and summons each Bella, one by one.

"I think I have a shot at winning, don't you?" I ask when my turn comes.

Joanne shrugs in her Joanne way. "Depends how everyone else does. Get on the scale."

I start unlacing my running shoes. "I weighed you with shoes on last time," she says. "No cheating. Keep them on."

My heart soars at the sight of the digits between my feet. "I lost eleven pounds!" I crow.

"Don't get your panties in a bunch," Joanne says. "This is about fat loss, not just weight."

"What panties?" I say.

"Funny," Joanne says. "Drop them so I can measure you."

The first two times Joanne measured me, she shocked unshockable me. It just felt wrong, standing naked in a bathroom at work with the company trainer wrapping a tape measure around my breasts and upper thighs—wrong enough that I'd insisted on keeping my underwear on while Joanne measured me. Now it barely fazes me to drop my Lulus to my ankles—until I see Joanne's mouth drop in horror.

"What's that mess?" she yelps, pointing a tiny finger at my pubes.

I regard the offensive situation. "I guess I haven't gotten waxed for a while."

"*Waxed?* Who gets waxed anymore? You need to get that shit lasered off if you're ever going to get any action in this town."

"All of it?"

"Jesus, girl. No one has *pubic hair* anymore."

Still shaking her head, Joanne continues taking my measurements, pinching my upper arm with a metal caliper, clamping the cold metal onto my thigh, my belly, my butt. She enters each number into her phone.

"Get dressed," she says, running a bacterial wipe over her calipers.

"How'd I do?" I wheedle.

"You did good," she says. "Now go tell Heather I'm ready for her."

I ABSTAIN FROM FOOD for the rest of the day, just in case someone demands a recount. Finally the announcement appears in my inbox. "Oh my God," I whisper to myself, because it would be bad form to scream. "I won!"

Yes, I had an unfair advantage—the contest rewards a change in body fat, not the lowest percentage of body fat. Unlike my co-workers, I actually had fat to lose. But still: I'm the oldest Bellissima employee by twenty years. Not to mention a contender for Most Likely to Comfort Herself with Emotional Eating. And I promised myself I'd win. And I won, dammit. I won.

TEN

After working at Bellissima for a year I've saved some money, but I haven't saved my marriage. So now I'm going to spend most of what I've saved getting divorced.

Wishful thinking is all that's left of my hope. It's been years since my wife and I shared tender words. Years since I took a breath without pain. I'm desperate for resolution. I want to live one day and then another without this strangled throat, this aching chest. Taking a step has to land me someplace better. I hire a gay family-law attorney. On the phone with him the first time, I can barely spit out the word *divorce*.

Filing for divorce so soon after finally winning the right to be married—and only four years after my wife and I tied the legal knot—I feel that I'm betraying more than my vows. I'm betraying my own beliefs about social change *and* marriage. In many cities over many years, I marched for marriage equality. I argued with the Prop H8ers and I argued with the gay people who said that marriage would co-opt us, diminish us, turn our imaginative, quirky queer culture into a caricature of miserable, boring, heterosexual married life.

"You're not filing for the first gay divorce, and yours won't be the last," my lawyer says.

I write him a big check. He e-mails me a big pile of documents. I print them out after work. The folder I put the pages in is nearly an inch thick. I go home and put the folder on the dining table, right next to the vase where I keep cheerful sprays of magenta bougainvillea, clipped from the bush outside my door.

I approach and avoid the folder for a day, a week, a month. In Al-Anon they say, "Don't quit before the miracle." I'm waiting for the miracle. I'm waiting to wake up happily married and tell my wife about my horrible dream.

My lawyer leaves me a message about the paperwork. I don't call him back or fill it out. He calls a second time.

The miracle isn't coming. I'm not going to wake up from this bad dream. So I go home to my crappy apartment with nothing of mine in it and my name alone on the lease, and I force myself to open the folder and pull out the first page.

There it is, for the last time ever: my wife's name on an official document right next to mine.

IN 1996, when my wife and I fell in love, getting legally married wasn't something two women could do. We didn't let that get in our way.

We bought wedding rings five months after our first night together. We weren't quite ready to do the deed, but buying the rings staved off our shared sense of urgency. I didn't know then what I'd learn later in Al-Anon: "If it feels urgent, it probably isn't important. If it's important, it probably doesn't feel urgent." I didn't know then that twenty years later I'd be combing through this happy memory and every happy memory asking myself, Is this where we went wrong? Or was it there?

In 1999, thanks to the persistence of a lesbian state assembly-woman, domestic partnership became available to same-sex couples in California. "DP" was a pale shadow of real marriage, but it was there to do, so of course we hurried up and did it.

For the next five years we kept the rings in their red velvet jeweler's box in my underwear drawer. On our six-year anniversary we retrieved the box and went out for mani-pedis and cheap Chinese food, and came home and read the vows we'd written to each other, and slipped the wedding bands onto each other's ring fingers, and poured two flutes of Veuve.

"My wife forever," she toasted us.

"My wife forever," I agreed.

Friends saw the rings and protested our elopement. They wanted to celebrate with us. One year after we married ourselves by ourselves, we were married again at a friend's home in the calm, closed mouth of Tomales Bay. Everyone we loved was there. Everyone who loved us. My wife's godson stood in for her father. It wasn't my first wedding, but for the first and last time, my dad walked me down the aisle.

IN 2004, when gay marriage was suddenly legal in the City of San Francisco, I was midway through a month-long writers' residency in upstate New York. My wife begged me to fly home and stand in the rain with her and thousands of grooms and grooms and brides and brides in the line that snaked around and around City Hall. I'd applied to this residency eleven times before I finally got in. I had a book deadline I'd miss if I took my eyes off the ball for even a day. Sadly, I told my wife I couldn't come home.

A few days later, when the City of New Paltz, New York, started offering wedding licenses to same-sex couples, I asked my wife to fly east and marry me there. Laughing, we came up with a compromise plan. My wife went online and booked us a date to be legally married in the San Francisco City Hall Rotunda, the day after I got home.

But then an e-mail to every same-sex couple with a San Francisco wedding date.

By order of the California Supreme Court, the San Francisco County Clerk has been ordered to discontinue issuance of same-sex marriage licenses. Therefore, all previously scheduled same-sex appointments are now canceled.

"I wanted to *really* marry you," my wife cried into the phone. "I wanted to really marry you, too," I cried.

ON MAY 15, 2008, the California Supreme Court ruled, "An individual's sexual orientation—like a person's race or gender—does not constitute a legitimate basis upon which to deny or withhold legal rights."

Gay marriage was legal again in California. Gay people danced in the streets. My wife and I had plenty of time now to plan a real wedding. This time the Supreme Court had ruled. What could possibly go wrong? We raised a quick toast and returned to our posts at Obama campaign headquarters, conveniently located in a storefront two blocks from our house.

We'd spent many happy hours in that filled-to-bursting room, making calls and planning fundraisers and hearing the stories of our elderly African American neighbors, who'd paid the poll tax to vote in Texas or Mississippi decades ago, and now were about to elect the first black president of the United States.

"I never thought . . ." a white-haired, stooped-over woman said, shaking her church-hatted head.

"Not in our lifetimes," the man next to her agreed.

I made the phone calls and ate the homemade mayonnaise cake and drank the Mr. Coffee with hazelnut creamer and divided up the call lists, swelling with love for my wife, our neighborhood, our country, and, for once, our president-to-be.

We were so excited about electing Obama, we weren't paying attention when the backlash against gay marriage became a Catholic-and-Mormon-funded movement. We weren't paying attention when the movement became Prop 8, a ballot measure to overturn the new law. It'll never pass, we reassured each other as Election Day approached. We called it Prop H8. California would never let right-wing religious fanatics steal our shiny new right.

The week before Election Day, our inboxes were flooded with gay friends' wedding invitations. "Just in case Prop 8 passes," they explained. Several used the phrase *shotgun wedding*. The *San Francisco Chronicle* ran a story about civilians being deputized by the dozens as "Marriage Commissioners for a Day" to handle the load.

Two nights before Election Day, my wife and I were cleaning up after dinner, watching Rachel Maddow as usual, so we didn't miss a bit of good Obama news. But the news that night wasn't good. Thanks to organized homophobia's gazillion-dollar ad campaign, and confusion about whether a yes vote meant yes to gay marriage or yes to abolishing gay marriage, Proposition 8 was predicted to win.

"Let's get married," my wife said. She put down her dish towel and put her arms around me. "Let's get married right now."

EARLY THE NEXT MORNING, just before our twelfth anniversary and the day before the 2008 election, my wife and I put on our *No on 8* T-shirts and our best jeans and favorite feather boas and put our witnesses, my mother and William and Armando, into my car and drove downtown to the Alameda County Clerk-Recorder's Office. The lobby was a Gay Pride party, pulsating with ecstatic couples, male and female, pushing strollers and pushing walkers, wearing wedding dresses and dressed in drag, laughing and crying with joy. The beleaguered city clerks were signing specially issued licenses as fast as they could. The women got licenses with two spaces marked "Bride." The men's licenses had two spaces marked "Groom."

Finally, finally. My wife and I stood beneath an arbor of grimy yellow plastic daisies and green plastic ivy in the county chapel in front of a hastily deputized marriage commissioner, who confided, before stepping behind the podium, that he'd volunteered for the job because his closeted gay brother had died twenty years ago of AIDS. We were his eleventh marriage of the day, he said, and it was only 10:30 a.m.

"It's a big day," he said solemnly. "Everyone's worried about what might happen tomorrow."

He turned to my wife and me. "Are you ready?" he asked.

Holding each other's hands, we nodded.

"Will you take this woman to be your wedded wife, to live together in the state of matrimony? Will you love, honor, and keep her, in sickness and in health, and forsaking all others, keep yourself only unto her, as long as you both shall live?"

"I will," my wife said, beaming at me with tears running down her face.

"I will," I said, beaming at her.

THE NEXT NIGHT, my wife and I stood in the Oakland Convention Center, shoulder to shoulder with hundreds of other Obama volunteers, watching on the Jumbotron as our Obama dream came true.

When Barack and Michelle Obama lifted their clasped hands above their heads and beamed down at us from the huge screen, we cheered and cried and danced with our fellow volunteers. For the first time in my life, my country actually seemed sane to me, in sync with reality, in sync with my beliefs.

A few hours later, the headline on the Jumbotron read "Proposition 8 Passes in California." My wife and I clutched each other, devastated, as many of the people around us cheered. We knew our fellow campaigners were churchgoers, and we knew their churches had been proselytizing about "saving marriage," but still. How could we share such passion for Obama and be at war about love?

At midnight my wife and I drove home through Oakland streets exploding in celebration. The amazingly good news: we had a new president, the first one either of us had ever wanted. The not-so-good news: the people who had elected our new president had also changed our marital status from "married" to "unknown."

ALSO UNKNOWN: why, two months after the happiest day of our lives, the happiest day of our twelve years together, I looked into my wife's eyes and found a stranger's cold disinterest where my wife's bright, loving gaze used to be. Why should legal marriage turn two people who have been in love with each other for more than a decade, two people who have already married each other in every way they could, into enemy combatants?

In my desperation I scoured the Internet and discovered a string of studies conducted after the passage of Prop 8. One concluded that "the mental health outcomes of gays and lesbians would improve if laws such as Proposition 8 did not exist because . . . laws that say to gay people 'you are not welcome here, your relationships are not valued,' have 'significant power.'" Another found that gay people in states where same-sex marriage had been outlawed "had the highest reports of 'minority stress'—the chronic social stress that results from minority-group stigmatization—as well as general psychological distress."

Gay bodies suffer, too. A study by Emory University economists found increased rates of HIV infection in states that had banned same-sex marriage—and a decrease in doctor visits among Massachusetts gay men after that state lifted the ban.

The studies didn't help me understand where my wife and I went wrong. I knew only that our trouble started shortly after the happiest day of both of our lives. And it never stopped.

SO NOW, DIVORCE.

I put all the papers back into the folder and I take the folder to the nearest Starbucks. I know I'll never want to go back to the place where I fill out these forms, and Starbucks isn't a place I'll miss.

PETITION FOR

_x_ Dissolution   ___Legal Separation   ___Nullify.

LEGAL RELATIONSHIP (Check all that apply)

_x_ We are married.

_x_ We are domestic partners.

LEGAL GROUNDS based on (Check one)

_x_ Irreconcilable differences.

___Permanent legal incapacity.

___Incest.

___Bigamy.

SPOUSAL OR DOMESIC PARTNER SUPPORT

___Spousal or domestic partner support payable to

___Petitioner

___Respondent

For the first time since my wife and I met, I'm earning more money than she does. So I got the right to be married just in time to get divorced, and now I'm going to have to pay *alimony*? I step outside Starbucks to call my lawyer.

"Did you hear the great news?" he answers.

"What great news?"

"The U.S. Supreme Court just overturned DOMA!"

"What?"

"Gay marriage is now legal in every one of the United States! We finally get all the federal benefits of marriage! This is true marriage equality!"

I turn this over in my mind. "So . . . just when I started getting divorced, the Supreme Court made me more married?"

My lawyer, who happens to be happily gay-married, sighs into the phone. "I guess it's not such great news for you personally," he says. "Actually, your divorce is probably going to cost you more because of this decision." He pauses. "It might take longer, too, because no one understands the legal implications yet."

I imagine my lawyer and his husband, and all the suddenly federally married couples, celebrating their great news. Never have I fought so hard for a change that hurt me so much.

"At least we won," I say, feeling like the opposite of a winner.

ELEVEN

Your dad fell." Lina is crying into my phone. "I couldn't pick him up."

It's rush hour on a Friday. It'll be faster to drive. I jump into my car and go. I've got the drill down: heavy foot on gas pedal; eyes darting between the asphalt unspooling in front of me, the rearview mirror for cop-watching, and the sky, to which I address my prayers.

Lina calls as I'm summiting the Grapevine. "False alarm," she says. "He's okay. I didn't even have to take him to the hospital. Are you already on your way?"

Thanks, God. "I'll be there in four hours." I don't have to explain why I'm not turning around. Lina hasn't left my dad's side in weeks.

The apartment has the sour stench of a hospital room. I kiss my stepmother and my brother and say hello to my dad's hospice nurse. My father is sleeping, flat on his back on his gray leather recliner, up to his chin in a blue plaid wool blanket I remember from our family's early days in New York. How did that blanket make it here through everything that's happened in between: my parents' divorce in the early seventies, my father's second marriage and divorce, his marriage to Lina, their moves from New York to London to Bermuda to this final address?

The blanket looks exactly the same. Not so my dad. The silver stubble of his beard, gently shaved each morning by Lina, glints against his pale gray face. I sink onto the carpet, back against his chair.

"Hello, sweetheart," my dad says.

I scramble onto my knees, which puts us at eye level. "Hello, Pops."

My dad smiles at me, and the whole six-decade story of us is in that smile. We've been best friends and worst enemies; we've walked away from each other, screaming accusations; we've returned to each other again and again.

My dad was the tyrant who ruined my teenage life. He forbade me to travel below Fourteenth Street or above Ninety-sixth, to watch TV or talk on the phone or see my friends. He threatened to have my first, English boyfriend deported and forbade me to see every boyfriend after that until I ran away to Taos with the first one I really loved. When I was thirty-three, joyously in love with my first girlfriend, my father banned her from family gatherings, called our relationship "illegitimate," and advised me to see a psychiatrist to cure my "homosexual infatuation." I yelled at him. He yelled at me. I hung up on him. He hung up on me. For the next eight years, we didn't speak.

And then somehow, during the death-knell years of my marriage, that guy and his wife became my trusted confidants. Their apartment became my refuge, the place I went to be listened to and fed and understood.

All the painful bumping around my dad and I did for our first sixty years is over now. There will be no more arguing about whose version of our story is true. We know how the story ends, and we know when: very, very soon. All that's left for my dad and me now is pure, uncomplicated love.

My dad reaches over the arm of the recliner and takes my hand. My heart soars. My father has slapped me and patted me but he's never touched me affectionately, ever. I shuffle a bit closer to his chair so he won't let go.

I feel my dad's discomfort about holding his daughter's hand, and I feel that he wants to hold it. I wonder if he has ever wanted to hold my hand before, or hug me, or kiss me. I wonder what stopped him then. I know what's making it possible for him to do it now.

MY DAD IS DYING, and my dad is holding my hand. My dad has been far from a perfect dad, and right now he's holding my hand.

My dad puts my hand palm down on his chest, not far from his heart. He starts tapping the top of my hand with the palm of his. I think he'll stop, but he doesn't. He starts talking to me, not in his usual booming New York Jewish voice, but quietly. So quietly I have to lean in to hear him.

"I was a terrible father," he says.

My eyes burn. How long have I waited for this apology? All my life. I don't want it now.

"I've been a terrible daughter," I say.

Pat, pat, pat. "You had your moments," my father says.

We regard each other warily, poised for ancient battle. His brown eyes have gone milky blue, the color of my babies' eyes when they were born. How could a father of mine have blue eyes? The same way my kids could, I guess: one foot in this world, one foot in another. No wonder he's speaking in the past tense.

My dad's eyes crinkle. A familiar spark lights them. He laughs.

"You had your moments," he repeats, and we laugh together. There's no one else I laugh with this way. When you go, I tell my dad silently, part of me goes, too.

Pat, pat, pat. "You need to let people come to you," my dad says, suddenly serious.

"What do you mean?"

"You underestimate yourself. You think you have to fight to get people's attention, but you don't. You're a remarkable person, Meredith. Stop fighting. Just be yourself. People will come to you."

My father dispensing advice like this—loving, calm, generous— is as rare a gift from him as touch. It makes me nervous. It's so not him. It's something he'd do only if he knew he'd never have to do it again, or be reminded that he'd done it once.

"Are you going all Wise Dad on me all of a sudden?" I say, try-ing to drag him back into our usual banter.

My father's expression doesn't change. "I'm sure my deficiencies as a father have a lot to do with your problems. I'm sorry for that."

What a time to find out what my father thinks my problems are. "Problems?" I say.

Pat, pat, pat. "I wish you saw yourself the way I see you," he says. "And I wish I'd told you before now."

"Told me what?"

"How wonderful you are." Pat, pat, pat. "You're smart and funny and you're a hard worker and you're kind. You're a good writer. Anyone would be lucky to know you."

I swallow hard, choking back tears.

"Being a parent is such a hard job," my dad goes on. "No one tells you what to do. It's the most important thing I ever did. I didn't know that until it was too late."

"You gave me so much, Dad," I say. "I'm a writer because of you. And—"

"I should have paid more attention to you and your brother. In my day, that's not what fathers did. But that's no excuse."

Funny, that's what I've always told my therapists. *Just because the other fifties fathers were assholes, that's no excuse.* Now it seems like a perfectly reasonable explanation. Like my father, most of my friends' dads ruled their families without deigning to engage in their day-to-day functioning. Why did I expect my father to transcend the dictates of time and place?

Some fathers did. I clung to the ones I found. I chose my third-grade best friend, Elaine, for her dad, a newspaper cartoonist who worked from home. Dave was as involved with Elaine's life as her mom was—maybe more. He had a sports car and he drove us around Washington Heights after school, two squealing eight-year-old girls squeezed into the tiny backseat of his forest-green MG.

"Your brother," my dad says. "He's the kind of father I wish I'd been. He's such a great dad. And you're such a terrific mother."

"I don't know . . ."

"See what I mean?" Pat, pat, pat. "You've got to start seeing the good in yourself."

My father's voice is louder, suddenly. He pats my hand harder and faster.

"I won't always be around to remind you," he says.

It seems ridiculous now, but I haven't actually thought this through. My dad won't be the first to call me when my byline appears in his morning newspaper. My dad won't be around to tell me the same boring, self-aggrandizing, comforting stories he's been telling me all my life.

I'll still come to this apartment to see Lina, but my dad won't look up, delighted, as I walk through the door. Who else is as pleased by my presence as my father is? No one. Who likes me as much as he does, just the way I am? Only this guy, once my harshest critic, now my greatest fan. I want sixty more years of *this*.

"Take care of Lina, okay?" my father says. "You know she never asks for help."

"We will."

"She thinks you're all going to drop her when—"

"We won't."

My father closes his eyes. He stops patting my hand, but he leaves his hand, soft and hot and heavy, resting on mine. I close my eyes, too, telling myself to be here now with him, not in the future without him.

My dad startles like an infant. He jerks alert, eyes panicky.

"What about your marriage?" he asks.

Arrow to my heart. I can't lie to him. I can't give him the good news he wants. I have the craziest fantasy: my dad calls my wife and tells her that his dying wish is for us to get back together, and it works.

"We're getting divorced," I say.

"Oh, no. Why don't you try marriage counseling?"

Here's the dad I know, suggesting the obvious as if it's genius, trying to talk me into taking his advice. The last time he gave me words of wisdom like these, I was bemoaning my financial woes and he said, "Can't you put your politics aside, for once, and write a bestseller?" His advice-giving has always felt like it's more about easing his anxieties, making him feel like a hero, than it was about helping me. Now that distinction seems utterly insignificant.

"It's not going to happen, Dad. I already filed for divorce."

"Oh." He draws his lips together, a tight white line. I've disappointed him. Again.

"I'm sorry. I know you love her. I love her, too." My belly sends up a small flare of familiar anger. This is *my* divorce, *my* pain. I'm his daughter, not his mother. Why is it my job to make him feel better about it?

Because I want him to die in peace.

"We tried," I say.

"I know you did." My father's face softens. He looks . . . *thoughtful*. This is not a face I've seen on my father before.

"Dad. Couples counseling isn't a miracle cure. You're not married to anyone you went to couples counseling with. Neither am I."

"How did I get such a smart daughter?" He starts patting my hand again. "I'm sorry, sweetheart. Sometimes you can't have the thing you want most. But you can still have a lot of good things. And you will."

His eyelids droop. "Whatever happens," he mumbles, "make sure you keep writing. No one can take that away from you."

"I will."

"Promise me," says my father, who wrote dozens of unproduced plays until my mother got pregnant with me and he stopped writing to support his family, because that's what responsible fathers did in 1951. He didn't have the advantage I had, coming of age in the question-everything 1960s.

"I promise," I say.

"I'm leaving you a little bit of money to build yourself a place to write," my dad says.

This must be the dementia talking. My brother and I assumed that Lina would inherit whatever savings our father had, which was as it should be. Lina is seventy, with no other means of support.

"I love you, Dad," I say, for maybe the tenth time ever. Why haven't I said that to him every damn day of my life?

"I love you, too, sweetheart," my father says. Why has he never said that to me before?

I talk to God most of the way back to Los Angeles. Thank you for this miracle, I tell Him. Begging Him to keep my dad alive seems unrealistic. Instead I pray that my dad's slide out of this world is smooth and easy, and that his next world is full of calorie-free, mile-high pastrami sandwiches and winning bets.

A FEW DAYS LATER my brother calls. He's crying.

"Dad's gone," he says.

His voice seems to be coming through a long metal tunnel. "I'll be right there," I say.

Without saying anything to anyone, I gather my things and

walk out of the office. I get into my car and drive toward the 5. The traffic is worse than usual. I look at my dashboard clock. It's rush hour.

I call my stepmother. "It's over. Finally, it's over." Her voice is frozen. "He went peacefully. For him, this is better. But for us . . ."

"I know," I say. "I'm on my way. I love you."

I call my wife's cell phone. At least one thing, her phone number, is the same. She doesn't answer. She probably thinks I'm calling about the divorce. I leave her a message. "My father just died." I don't know what else to say. "I thought you'd want to know."

I call my therapist and leave her the same message.

My brother calls again. He's not crying now. I am.

"I don't think you should drive right now," my brother says. "It's getting dark. And you're upset."

I pull over to the curb. I see that my gas tank is almost empty. The thought of finding a gas station, finding my credit card, pumping gas is overwhelming. I ask God what to do. He says my brother's right.

"Okay," I say. "I'll leave first thing in the morning."

"No hurry," my brother says pointedly. "Drive safe."

Now what?

I'm sitting in my car on Sunset near Vine and I have no idea what to do, where to go.

My dad isn't alive anymore.

What does that even *mean*? I want to call my stepmother, tell her to put him on the phone so I know he's still on earth, where I need him to be.

I read somewhere that when people die, their souls hang around for a while. I close my eyes. I feel that my dad is still with me. Or maybe that's God. What if the God who's been holding me was actually my dad, and now my dad is gone?

I ask whichever of them is listening, "What do I do now?"

I feel him—my dad or God—tell me not to be alone.

I want to be with someone I really know and love, and I don't really know anyone in this town. To be specific, I want to be with my wife, who adored my dad, and whom my dad adored.

Outside my car window, a homeless woman slowly pushes a shopping cart across the intersection of Sunset and Vine. Drivers scissor around her, nearly hitting her, honking angrily. She doesn't look up or stop. Finally, she reaches the curb. She tips her cart up onto the sidewalk and stops next to my car, bent over her pile of rags. I start my car. I drive until I can't see her in my rear-view mirror anymore.

Cheap trick, I accuse God. If that was your way of reminding me that other people have it worse than I do, it's not working.

My dad isn't alive anymore.

My wife isn't my wife anymore.

I'm not anyone's anyone anymore.

I must know *someone* in Los Angeles. I scroll through the recent calls on my phone, trying to remember who I know. Hannah would be wonderful, but she's on the Westside. At this time of day, she might as well be in New York. Nichole and Donna? I dial their home number. Donna answers on the first ring.

"My father died," I say. "Can I—"

"Come right now," she says. "Do you need us to pick you up?"

The two of them are waiting at their front door. They pull me into a three-way hug. Holding them is like holding on to an oak tree. They walk me into their pale, calm living room. Donna hands me a cocktail and sits on the couch right next to me. "Dinner in a few," Nichole calls from the kitchen.

Donna puts her arm around me. "How are you, honey?"

I shake my head silently. Donna nods as if I've said the world's wisest thing.

"It's a terrible thing, losing a parent," she says. "It's like losing your place in the world."

My phone rings. "Oh my God," I say, staring at the number on the screen. "It's my wife."

"Answer it!" Donna says, and I do.

"HI," I SAY, in the voice that only my wife has heard.

"Hi," my wife says, in the voice she uses only with me.

Nichole and Donna are sweet and kind, and so new to me. Who could deeply comfort me in this moment? Only my wife. My wife who laughed at my father's dumb jokes, thanked him for making me, always told me I had his beautiful lips. The day after my wife and I met for the first time, my dad and I reconciled after our eight-year estrangement. My wife knew only the happy story of my dad and me. "The two of you are practically the same person," she said when she met him, naming our blessing and our curse.

I'm dimly aware of Donna walking me to their office, settling me into an easy chair, covering me with an impossibly soft blanket. She puts a box of Kleenex in my lap and closes the door behind her.

"I'm so sorry," my wife says. "He was a good guy, your dad."

Just as it always did, her voice pulls me in from where I've been drifting, anchors me to earth. *Is this the trade-off? I lose my father, but I get to hear my wife's voice?*

It was her voice that first caught me. Melodic, sexy, smart. And mysterious, always mysterious. Following her sideways thoughts, her poetic phrases, felt like tracing a curving path through a secret garden. I never knew what I'd come across, rounding the next bend, only that it would be surprising and beautiful and wild.

How can such a terrible thing and such a wonderful thing be happening at the same time? My father is dead. And I'm having a conversation with my wife, speaking the long-lost language of us.

"If you think it'll be okay with your family," my wife says, "I'd like to come to the memorial."

Her voice fills the hole in my heart. "Really?" I weep. "You'll come?"

WE CELEBRATE MY DAD with his idea of a perfect day, at the racetrack with every member of his family and the closest possible approximation of his favorite racetrack foods. We sit in his spot in the cheap seats and eat two-inch-tall pastrami and coleslaw sandwiches and tomato pickles like the ones he used to get at the Gaiety in Times Square, and dollar hot dogs and beer from the greasy grandstand shack. Sierra, his seven-year-old great-granddaughter, wins twenty bucks on a long shot. We all agree that this is Grandpa's work.

My wife texts me to say she's in the parking lot. I run to meet her. When she sees me, she stands still and waits. She wraps her arms around me, holds me long and close. I close my eyes and hold my breath. I'm home at last. All I want is to stay right here.

I hear a thin voice calling my wife's name. It's Sierra, galloping in our direction. She pries us apart, leaps into my wife's arms. Whenever my wife and I stayed at her parents' house, Sierra jumped into bed with us in the mornings.

"I miss you!" Sierra cries, burying her face in my wife's neck.

"I miss you, too, sweetie," my wife says.

God? Or my father? I don't care. Here's the miracle I've been waiting for.

TWELVE

Driving back to L.A. the day after my dad's memorial, I feel an old weight lifted and a new weight laid down.

There's no need to worry about my father anymore. No check-in calls to make to Lina or to his doctors, no scouring the web, researching his latest symptoms. There's nothing to do about my dad now except feel it: he's gone.

The miles blur by. Already the world feels quieter, lonelier, grayer without my father in it.

I turn on the radio. Mexican *corridos,* country and western ballads, Top 40, the audiobooks I stash in my glove box for these L.A.–San Francisco treks. One rattles me more than the next. I turn the radio off, summon my short list of self-soothing strategies, starting with focusing on the bright side.

No more suffering for my dad.

No more caretaking overload for Lina.

No more panicked phone calls or emergency trips to San Francisco for me.

No more seeing my father's face light up when I walk into a room.

Hello, God? It's me, Meredith. Where's my serenity?

PASSING GILROY, even through the closed car windows, I'm inhaling garlic air. It's always like this, passing Gilroy. Summer or winter, rain or shine. Drive past Gilroy, smell garlic. Why do some things, stupid things that don't even matter, stay the same, but the most important things, the best things, won't?

Change the channel. Think of something good.

My wife yesterday, in the racetrack parking lot with her arms around me. The familiar scent of her skin.

My wife.

I want more of that.

I phone my wife.

I listen to her outgoing message. It's good to hear her voice. I don't know what's going to happen between us, but I do know this: She showed up for me. She still loves me. And I still love her. I leave her a message. "Just thinking of you on Highway 5."

I slip into a reverie. Maybe we'll start talking again. Forgive each other. She'll come to L.A. to visit me.

I imagine my wife in my little Silver Lake deprivation cell. In my lonely exile bed. Pulling her to me. Kissing her. Both of us saying it again and again. *I'm sorry, my love. I'm sorry.*

Five hours later I pull into my alley, shoehorn my car into my tiny garage, emerge into the balmy L.A. night. The 7-Eleven compressors are still chugging. The purple bougainvillea still pours over the fence. So much has changed since I left L.A. three days ago.

I call my wife again. I get her voice mail again. I leave her a message, thanking her for her kindness, asking her to call me back when she's ready. I know she needs her space. The way she came through for me makes it easier to give it to her. I squeezed her too tightly when we were married, I know I did. But now I've walked through the fire. I've been alone. I'm not so needy anymore. I can do better than I did before. She'll see.

LOSS IS A SLOW, slow walk. I've been sad about my dad for a long time. Now I miss him every day. I wish he could have lived another five, ten, thirty years. But his death fits into the natural order of things. A daughter is supposed to outlive her father. A daughter hurts her father and makes him happy, and he does the same to her. We forgave each other and thanked each other, and then he slipped from here to there.

Losing my marriage is different. Worse. When I lost my wife I lost the person I was with her. I lost the woman and the life I loved. I lost the history my wife and I made together, the future I'd counted on, the future we'd planned to share.

Accept the things you cannot change; change the things you can. Unlike losing my father, losing my wife is something I might be able to change. Living without both of them feels impossible. So I'm going to try to get my wife back. I'm going to try.

WHEN I WAKE UP in the morning I leave my wife a message. "Just saying hi."

The next day I call my wife from work and leave her a message. "Call me when you can."

I e-mail my wife at bedtime the next night. "Left you some voice mails. Haven't heard back. Hope you're okay."

Days go by. I don't hear from her.

She's having drinks with friends on Facebook.

Weeks go by. She's on a beach in France.

Months go by. I don't hear from her.

I'M UNTETHERED AGAIN, drifting through space. How deluded was I, interpreting a moment of shared grief as a reconciliation. My wife and I are not getting back together. What we're getting is divorced.

The *V* in that word: that's my wife and me. Two sides, joined at the bottom, broken apart at the top. My magical thinking can't put us back together again. My marriage is over. It's time to face my demons, my new life, my future. Alone.

A YEAR AFTER I MOVED to L.A., my wife e-mails to say she's moving out of the house we lived in together, the house I own. She takes the things that are hers alone and leaves everything else, pending our legal settlement.

I call Naomi, my Bay Area realtor. She tells me the real estate market is smoking hot. "But you have to get your house on the market *now*," Naomi says. "No one buys a house in Oakland in August. Can you empty it in the next two weeks?"

"Of course," I lie. I haven't set foot inside that house since the day I left for L.A., and it's full of twenty-five years' worth of stuff.

I call Celia, my best and most grounded friend. "Two words," she says. "Yard sale."

"You mean get rid of all my stuff?"

"What else are you going to do with it?" Celia says.

"It's everything I have."

"Everything you *had*."

"I could rent a storage unit."

"Until when?"

"Until I get a bigger place."

"Honey." In the first twenty years of our friendship, Celia never used this stern, maternal tone with me. In the past couple of years, she's used it a lot.

"You've been saying for years that you want to live in a small place." Celia's voice softens. "Emptying your house is going to be really hard. But hanging on to your stuff isn't going to make it any easier."

I take a quick mental inventory of the contents of the ten rooms in my Oakland house. The down couch my wife and I designed together, flipping through swatch books, picking the perfect assemblage of fabrics and then an even more perfect combination. The antique table I found on the street when my husband and I were newly married and broke, then stripped until its purple paint surrendered to gleaming mahogany. The red leather recliner I bought because I thought it would make my writing better and never used. The bed my dad gave us as a wedding gift.

The bed . . .

Looking back on this past year of living thinglessly, I can

count on one hand the inanimate objects I've reached for and wished I still had. My grease-splattered, tie-dyed Ben & Jerry's apron. My wooden-handled potato scrubber. A pair of earrings that were a birthday gift from Cori, my best friend since middle school. My beat-up *Roget's Thesaurus,* even though for years now, since my grip on words has been loosening, I've been finding my synonyms online.

On the list of what I've been missing, *things* just don't deserve a place at the top. It's a function of age, in part: instead of imagining all the pleasure each thing will bring me over the years I'll own it, I imagine my kids sifting through piles of stuff when I die. Like the rest of my ex-attachments and ex-realities, my connection to my things has changed.

"I'll come up next weekend," I tell Celia.

"I'll round up the crew," she says. "You're not doing this alone."

"How did I get so lucky, to have a friend like you?"

"You'd do the same for me." Celia pauses. "You've done it. As we both know."

Ten years ago, Celia was driving home on her motorcycle when she was broadsided by a Mercedes-Benz. During the nine weeks she spent in the ICU, one or more of our friends was stationed at her bedside most of the time. Although Celia doesn't remember any of it, she says she made a full recovery, against every doctor's prognosis, because we were there.

Then, three years ago, Celia was on a beach in Costa Rica with her husband, Brent, when he started struggling for breath. Just to be safe, Celia drove him to the local clinic. Six hours later, Brent was dead, and Celia was in a foreign country alone. She called me, and I called "the girls." When Celia flew home I picked her up at the airport, drove her to her house, and took Brent's place in their bed. Over the next weeks and months our crew body-guarded Celia, fed her, monitored her sleeping pill intake, drove her to her therapist's office, and rejoiced with her the first time she got through a day without breaking down.

This is long-term friendship as I know and need it. This is the difference between walking through life accompanied and walking through life alone. Sleeping next to Celia when her husband dies, being sheltered by Celia when my marriage goes up in flames.

Andrew Sullivan said it well in his 1988 essay collection, *Love Undetectable*. "Love comes quickly, as the song has it, but friendship ripens with time. If love is at its most perfect in its infancy, friendship is most treasured as the years go by."

MY E-MAIL INBOX starts pinging with proof that my Bay Area friends are running the show. Larissa photographs the contents of the house and posts the photos on craigslist. Laura offers to feed the team. Jasmine will take the money. My brother and his girlfriend lend their pricing expertise. Roland, who used to coach my son's basketball team, will bring some strapping young players to load the heavy stuff into my customers' cars. Alison will act as personal shopper, following potential buyers around, making sure they realize how much they need my stuff.

As it happens, that Sunday is the day Patricia's husband has planned her memorial. I'll hold my yard sale on Saturday only. Whatever goes, goes. Whatever doesn't goes to Goodwill.

———

THE SALE'S ADVERTISED START TIME is eight a.m. I find a knot of shoppers, their eyes wild with bargain lust, on the front porch at six.

My friends show up and take over. I feel like a shopper myself, wandering the rooms where my life used to be, picking up one object, setting it down, picking up another.

An old man with a blue Ikea shopping bag taps me on the shoulder. "Will you take ten for this?" he asks. I follow his eyes to the life-sized mirror on the wall. My wife and I called it "Patricia's mirror" because she swore it made her look taller and thinner. The night she died, I was lying on the down couch when the mirror suddenly fell—or jumped—off its hook and landed on the floor, intact.

"Sorry," I tell the man. "That mirror isn't for sale." And then I look around at the other things in the room. The leaded-glass cabinet my husband and I bought in a junk store as a wedding gift to ourselves. The wrought-iron lamp with the dancing angels that my wife and I found at a yard sale in Vancouver and carefully carried home. The clunky wooden KLH stereo speakers my first boyfriend and I bought in 1969 with the advance for the hippie-back-to-the-land book we wrote together. Am I really going to leave all these things behind?

I could tell my real estate agent that I'm not ready to sell, and spend the next year of weekends saying good-bye to every object in this house, wallowing in grief. Or I could rent a huge storage space and delay the sorting and wallowing. Or I can do what I promised Celia I'd do: let go of all of it and walk away.

"Will you take twenty?" the man with the Ikea bag presses me.

"It's yours," I say.

NINE HOURS LATER I have a thick wad of bills in my purse and five cardboard boxes—the survivors of the purge—in my car. I tell my crew to meet me at Gather, Celia's favorite Berkeley bistro. When we're settled into a booth, Celia proposes a toast. "To moving on."

We all raise our glasses. "To moving on," we say.

THE NEXT MORNING, Patricia's husband, Mark; her daughter, Maya; her dog, Blue; and a dozen of the people who cared for all of them convene at a trailhead in the Oakland hills. We walk the East Ridge Trail in silence, shadowed by towering eucalyptus, oaks, and redwoods, the path we used to hike with Patricia and Blue.

We gather at Patricia's favorite spot, a bench overlooking a canyon of scrub and blackberry bramble and twining poison oak. Daffodils are spring bloomers, but on this July day Patricia's bench is circled by a ring of nodding yellow trumpets.

Blue remembers. He jumps up onto the bench, barking and whining. "It's okay, Blue," Maya says again and again, until the dog relaxes into the girl's arms.

Mark pulls a cardboard box from his backpack. Tears coursing down his face, he recites the poem that Patricia wrote and spoke as her vows at their wedding. He lifts the lid with one hand, fills the other hand with his wife's ashes, and passes the box to their daughter, who does the same. Mark and Maya toss the ashes into the canyon, white powder and bone dusting the low-lying branches and gray-green leaves. "Good-bye, my love," Mark says, and Maya says, "Bye, Mom," and then Mark upends the box of ashes on Patricia's favorite patch of earth.

We trek back to the parking lot and huddle for a moment, hugging each other good-bye. As I head for my car, Olivia, Patricia's housecleaner, whom Mark entrusted with disposing of Patricia's possessions, approaches me with a bulging shopping bag. "Patricia told me to keep these for you," Olivia says, handing me the bag.

"Thank you." I take the bag to my car, close my eyes to have a quiet moment with Patricia, and then start pulling clothes out of the bag. My favorite dress of Patricia's. My favorite pair of her pants. A metallic blue purse I'd admired. I gasp, clutching the olive-green fleece jacket Patricia was wearing the day we met.

Yesterday I let go of everything from my old life. Today Patricia gave me a starter kit for the new.

My route back to L.A. takes me down the hill past Patricia's house, where we used to hang out in her immaculate chef's kitchen, drinking her good Manhattans and eating her good food and talking our good talk, and across the flatlands of Oakland, no longer my hometown, and onto the freeway south. Most of the things I owned two days ago when I left L.A., the stuff I accumulated in sixty years of living, aren't mine anymore. And I'm going home with things I didn't have two days ago, Patricia's things, new and precious to me.

———————

IT SEEMS A FITTING WAY to spend my second Independence Day in La-La: sitting on my rented living room floor, opening the boxes I brought from my Oakland house, soon, goddess willing, to be someone else's house; sorting my kids' decades-old artwork, turning the pages of our family photo albums. The happy scenes seem to have happened more than one lifetime ago: the early years, two tiny boys with mother and father, then little boys with father and stepmother and two mothers, then teenage boys with father, stepmother, stepsister, mother, and mother's wife. It's difficult, but I manage to restrain myself from opening the box of love letters from my wife.

With the entirety of my possessions spread before me, what was surreal days ago is suddenly real. Besides the empty house they came from and the few dresses hanging in my rented bedroom closet, this is all I own.

Now that I've loosened myself from my belongings, facing the rest of my new life without the net of my familiar things feels like walking a tightrope. Also, it makes me feel unburdened, unencumbered, free.

SINCE I LEFT SAN FRANCISCO, the tech boom has driven real estate prices sky-high. This has driven renters and buyers to the east side of the Bay, which has, in turn, driven many of my African American neighbors out. My Oakland neighborhood—which was listed as "ghetto adjacent" when I bought my home in 1989, and which some of my friends were afraid to visit, and which gave me neighbors and experiences and insights I never would have otherwise had—has been reclassified from dangerous to desirable.

My house sells ten days after it goes on the market, for three times what I paid for it twenty-four years ago. Escrow closes quickly. I walk away with almost twice as much money as I expected to clear.

This windfall is a game changer for me, and an identity changer, too. Since I left home as a teenager I've been a proud, scrappy member of the 99 percent. I've never gone hungry, but I've never stopped hustling to pay the mortgage, either. Now, suddenly, I have a job that pays me more than I need to live on, and enough cash to buy a house in another gentrifying neighborhood in another expensive city.

Who and what does that make me? Since high school I've been an activist whose worldview, lifestyle, and financial status were more outlier than mainstream. Through my decades as an antiwar radical, a back-to-the-land hippie, a factory worker and union organizer, a wife and mother, a gay rights advocate, an Occupier, a writer, I've always identified with the underdog and the marginalized. When a bad war started or a bad law passed, I voted with my feet, with my people, in the streets.

I came of age in a youth movement whose organizing principle was "Don't trust anyone over thirty" and a Dylan anthem that promised we'd be "Forever Young." As that milestone receded in my rearview mirror, I updated the mantra, rejecting the rumor that aging in itself makes people more conservative. That might have been true of previous generations, but it couldn't possibly be true of ours.

Taking stock now, I'm stunned to realize that in my year-plus as an Angeleno, I haven't been to a single demonstration. That's a first for me since 1966. Is that because I'm no longer young? Or because aging *has* made me care more about my own fate and care less—do less—about the world's?

Without kids to set an example for, without the whip of freelance insecurity, with a financial profile that situates me on the privileged side of the social balance sheet, how will I maintain my lifelong principles? Will I surrender to affluenza—stop afflicting the comfortable and comforting the afflicted—in favor of my own comfort? Will this new combo platter of financial ease and sixtysomething hindsight shift my allegiance, narrow my worldview, turn me into the kind of shallow materialist I swore I'd never be?

THIRTEEN

’ve never been a person who loves routine, and I left behind the few I had in Oakland a year ago. I do have one post-L.A. ritual, though, which helps me understand the appeal. Every Sunday morning, rain or shine (shine), I get out of bed at nine, step into a T-shirt, a pair of shorts, and my flip-flops, and walk the hills of Silver Lake to the Al-Anon meeting at the gay recovery center a mile away.

I love everything about this meeting. The greeter for the day, usually a hunky gay man, gives out big hugs at the door. I step inside the rainbow-festooned, window-lined room and make myself a cup of high-quality chai, or Earl Grey, or vanilla tea. The meeting is wildly popular. If I arrive early or on time, I usually find a free chair. If not, I’ll be standing in the kitchen doorway or squatting on the floor. It hardly matters. The meeting is a ride and we’re all rolling in the same direction, trying to “stay in our own lane,” keep the focus on ourselves instead of trying to change others, working at being unapologetically, serenely who we are.

One September Sunday on my walk home, I follow the yard-sale signs, playing "guess the demographic" as I go. Which sign will steer me to the moving sale of a Mexican family being gentrified out of the neighborhood? Which will lead me to the yard sales of gentrifiers like me, whose influx has cut Silver Lake's Hispanic population in half in the past fifteen years?

A succession of brightly hand-painted ART SALE signs leads me down the long driveway of a funky Craftsman cottage. Its double-lot garden is breathtaking, more Moroccan souk than Silver Lake backyard, divided into mini-galleries delineated by living walls of ficus trees. Canopied daybeds dressed in mirrored Indian fabrics perch on tiled platforms. A two-story-tall papier-mâché Jimi Hendrix plays a papier-mâché guitar. The garden's back wall is a Mexican-style mural depicting Mexican artists painting a mural. The cement path through the crazy maze is a modern-day mosaic, embedded with bottle caps and pennies and vintage marbles and pottery shards. The roof is a huge silk parachute hung from cactus trees.

A familiar sensation blooms in my throat, my belly, my chest. I remember that feeling. It's joy.

There's an upside to being so alone in this town, in this new life. I can take as long as I want, exploring this wonderland. My time is my own. No one is expecting me anywhere. I have nothing else to do, nowhere else to be.

Savoring each eyeful, I make my way through the labyrinth, kneeling to peruse a stack of primitive portraits rendered in hot tropical colors, signed Leticia Martinez. I pull out a tic-tac-toe grid of heart-shaped faces, half of them grinning happily, the others tearfully sad. The message speaks to me, and its pink, red, and teal palette will brighten my office at work. An older man in paint-splattered overalls approaches me.

"I'm Miguel," he says, giving me a warm grin. "How are you today?"

"Good," I answer reflexively, realizing to my surprise that it's true. "I love this painting. Do you know how much the artist wants for it?"

"Twenty?"

"Twenty *dollars*?"

"Okay, then," Miguel says. "Fifteen?"

"That's not enough!" I protest.

Miguel gestures at the stacks of canvases around us. "Leticia is very prolific. She's always happy when one of her paintings finds a good home."

I hand Miguel a twenty-dollar bill, tuck my new painting under my arm, and continue on my walk. The next sign I see says HOUSE FOR SALE. And the next thought I have is, This is my house.

It's tiny, a classic 1920s Spanish-style bungalow, stucco, with a flat terra-cotta tile roof. It's painted an awful pinkish color that clashes with its Wedgwood-blue trim. It can't possibly have more than one bedroom, and I need two—one for me, one for a guest room/office. I don't see a chimney, which means no fireplace. A fireplace is a must-have, too. So this cannot be my house.

But.

But my heart is racing, and I can't turn my head from this little bungalow with its wild jungle garden, a riot of purple Mexican sage and fuzzy red kangaroo paws and dusty aloe spikes and a white climbing rose. I swear the orange tree is holding out its arms to me. I peek inside the tall front windows. The house is flooded with L.A.'s magical golden light.

I call the number on the FOR SALE sign.

"Max Rosenman," a man answers.

"Hi. I'm interested in the bungalow on Micheltorena."

"Are you carrying a painting with hearts on it?" the man asks.

"Yes. How did you know that?"

"I live across the street," he says. "I can see you from here. I'll be right over."

A few seconds later a young guy with a full beard and a man bun, wearing no shirt, tattered gray sweat shorts, and flip-flops, walks across the street and unlocks the bungalow's door. I step into the living room. The front windows and front door face the downtown L.A. skyline, the vista filtered through a lemon tree's glossy green leaves.

"That's what they call a million-dollar view," Max says.

I nod, forcing myself to hide my excitement and my bargaining hand.

Max gives me a tour. It doesn't take long. The kitchen is tiny but sweet, with glass-faced cabinets and an old-school linoleum floor. The bathroom is small and ordinary, but the bathtub is long and deep.

Max leads me into the bedroom, where floor-to-ceiling French doors wash the room with more of that uplifting light. The doors open onto a long, narrow balcony that wraps around the back of the house. I've lived through four seasons in Los Angeles now, so I know I can put a daybed or a chaise on that balcony and spend weekends writing in the sun all year round.

"Wait till you see the best part!" Max leads me through the kitchen door and down a long outdoor stairway to a huge wooden deck shaded by the orange tree that welcomed me from the front.

"This space is a party waiting to happen." Max opens a door off the deck. "Bonus! Here's your guest room. Just needs a little work."

Inside another set of French doors is every writing-studio fantasy I've ever had: a small bathroom, a tiny galley kitchen, a bright bedroom with windows at eye level with the orange tree.

"What do you think?" Max asks me.

"I think I'm in love."

I've read a lot of L.A. real estate ads in the in this past year. I've been to lots of open houses with Clara, my decorator friend. With Clara's approval, I put in a couple of offers. I was more relieved than disappointed when the deals fell through. Although the houses were bigger, flashier, fancier than this one, I wasn't in love.

"Here's the craziest thing. Follow me." Max leads me up the stairs and through the kitchen and into the attached garage. Its walls are painted shocking pink and lined with industrial shelving. "The last renter was a set designer," Max says distractedly. "But check this out."

He points to a painting hanging on the garage wall. It's a smaller replica of the painting I'm still carrying, the one I bought at the art sale up the street a few minutes ago. The style is a bit different, but the message is the same: hearts in happiness, hearts in sorrow.

"I'm a painter. I did this one a year ago," Max says. "I put it up this morning. It's just like the one you're carrying! How cosmic is that?"

I put down my painting and I call Clara and then I call my realtor, Tina, and I ask them both to come over right now.

TWENTY MINUTES LATER I'm following Clara and Tina through the bungalow. Their faces tell me all I need to know.

"Wow," Tina says. "The light in here is incredible."

"It's small. And it needs some work," Clara says carefully. "But it's got good bones."

When I fall, I fall fast and hard. "Sold," I tell Max. "How soon can I move in?"

TWO WEEKS LATER, Tina meets me after work in the Bellissima parking lot. She hands me a cold bottle of Moët, a ring of keys, and an invitation to her birthday party next week, at a hot West Hollywood bar. "Cute girls," she promises with an exaggerated wink, and drives off.

I sit in my car with the two sets of keys in my hand. I only need one. I pull myself out of that thought, start my car, and drive fifteen minutes east to the bungalow—my bungalow. I open the front door and step into the living room and my heart sprouts wings. *I'm home.*

I sit on the living room floor, gazing out at the view. Behind the downtown L.A. skyline, the fiery sun melts into the horizon. The sky goes electric blue, smeared with finger-paint pink. *Show-off,* I scold God.

In the bedroom I pull open the tall casement windows, sit cross-legged on the splintery oak floor. The tallest branches of the orange tree brush the bottoms of the window frame, their sweet-tart scent perfuming the air. In the center of the vista, a red light atop a deco spire blinks rhythmically against the night. Through the palm trees to my left, office buildings are outlined in twinkling white lights. The thrill I've felt since the day I arrived in this city bubbles up inside me. *If I can make it here, I can make it anywhere.*

And I am. I am making it here.

AS IF TO REINFORCE this rare moment of Zen, there's a knock on the front door. It's Clara! My first visitor, dwarfed by an enormous wildflower bouquet.

She sets the vase down on the kitchen counter and hugs me. "Happy?" she asks.

Happy? Me? "I love this place so much," I say. It was good to be here alone. It's even better, sharing my excitement with a friend from my old life who's also a friend in my new life. "Have a seat," I say, offering her a prime spot on the floor.

"What are you thinking, decor-wise?" Clara asks, looking around.

"I thought I'd start by buying a bed. Then maybe a couch . . ."

"Want help?" Clara asks.

I've admired and copied Clara's design style as long as I've known her. "You know I can't afford you."

"I'll do it for cost. As a learning experience. Small houses are *huge* right now." Clara laughs. "If you don't mind being my guinea pig, it could work for both of us."

My heart lifts. "You have to let me pay you," I say. "My dad left me some money for exactly this purpose, to make sure I have a place to write. Also, for once in my life, I have a job."

"Whatever." Clara fishes a leather-bound graph pad and a silver pen out of her tote. "Tell me what you have in mind."

THE NEXT THREE WEEKS are a whirlwind of shopping and returning and repurchasing, before work and during work and after work and on weekends.

Mostly what I'm doing is saying yes to Clara. Yes to painting the living room walls a warm gray with white trim, and yes to painting the oak floors white to bounce all that sunlight around and make the Bungalito feel bigger. Yes to replacing the hollow-core doors with heavy oak French doors. Yes to making a bathroom vanity out of an old farm table, and yes to jumping into Clara's truck to cruise the used-furniture store for the table.

In my first marriage, my husband let me make all the decorating decisions. My first girlfriend and I, contentious in all matters, tried to decorate together, which translated to compromises that half-satisfied both of us. My wife and I moved through each renovation like a purring, beauty-making machine.

My collaboration with Clara is a different kind of partnership. The best and the saddest thing about it is that only one of us will end up living with the choices we're making together. We argue, but our arguments make us laugh. At a thrift store across the street from Bellissima, without Clara's approval, I find a red Formica coffee table in the shape of the state of California. I'm thrilled with my purchase. Clara, not so much.

"But it's *California*," I argue.

"I'm guessing your guests will know where they are without it."

"But it's *handmade*."

"So's the ashtray my kid made for me when she was seven," Clara says. "But I don't keep it in the middle of my living room."

"It's great for eating on. In case you hadn't noticed, there's no room for a dining table in here."

"Two words," Clara says. "Nesting tables."

The next day I come home from work to find the table in my driveway with a sign taped to it that says "Take me to the dump." I carry the table back to its rightful place in the living room. After work the next day I find it in the driveway again.

I tell Clara I love the table. Clara tells me how awful it is. We name the table "the battleground state."

Finally we reach a compromise. Clara agrees to let me keep the table if I'll move it to the deck, "where it'll rot long before I can convince you to get rid of it." Helena helps me carry the battleground state table to the deck, and Googles "nesting tables." The nicest ones she finds happen to be at a used Danish modern furniture store a few blocks away. "We can carry them home with our own little hands," she says, and so we do.

Incredibly, the work that needs to be finished before I move in—the painting of the walls and floors, the conversion of the garage, the installation of salvaged windows where walls once blocked views and light—is completed in exactly the allotted time for exactly the allotted budget. I relegate the improvements that can be done later—the design and installation of my dream garden, the new roof, the exterior paint, the purchasing of furniture— to a to-do list that isn't mine alone. Despite the paltry fee I'm paying her and the far more lucrative clients clamoring for her time, Clara promises to stick with me until every table and chair and lamp has been procured. I'm not a scrappy freelancer anymore; there's a paycheck replenishing my checking account every two weeks, so I can actually afford to buy them. All of this—the partnership with Clara, the salvage yards that offer up the perfect windows, the privilege of paying retail when retail is what's called for—seems nothing short of miraculous to me.

On my first night in my new home, I make my new bed with crisp new white sheets, a new, Los Angeles–weight duvet, and new goose-down pillows, and I lie in the middle of my bed and I watch the lights of downtown Los Angeles twinkling outside my windows until I fall into a fluffy sleep.

A call from Clara wakes me at dawn. "Look outside, quick!" she says.

I sit up in bed and see the cityscape through my south-facing windows, a tangle of jungle greenery and quirky Silver Lake cottages spilling down the hillside. The entire vista is doused in crimson light.

"This is the most beautiful sunrise I've ever seen," Clara says, "and it's happening just for you. Welcome home."

"I don't know how to thank you," I say.

"Be happy there," Clara says.

"I will," I say.

FOURTEEN

My L.A. friends declare my marital mourning period over and start dispensing Dr. Phil–style advice. "Move on with your life." "Put the past behind you." "Find someone new."

Find someone new? That's what I did the last time I was single. I was forty-five then. I'm past sixty now. What I need is someone old. Or someone willing to take a walk with someone old. For me, *moving on* means crossing a bridge away from my wife: leaving the land of us, pulling myself up onto a different shore. And crossing that bridge means making love—having sex, at least—with someone who isn't my wife.

Since I discovered sex, it's been everything to me. I started young and hope to stop never. Sex is where I connect with the body and the heart of the person I'm making love with. It's where I connect with the innermost essence of me. In lust, more than anywhere else, I find myself. Lose myself. Share myself. Am myself.

In non-sexual moments, when I'm pinballing around in my head, I can be anyone—wandering, spiraling, slipping on identities and shedding them. When I'm in my head I paint pretty pictures, spin scenarios real and imaginary, string together pretty words. But when I surrender to my animal hunger, when I lie down and reach deeply into another person, when I open myself to being reached, there's no mistaking me for anyone else.

As long as my wife remains the last person who touched me, the last person I touched, there will be no moving on. So I do what there is to do to change that. I join a dating site. I swallow my sadness—*how did this happen?*—and revulsion—*I'm too old and too smart for this shit*—and tackle the profile questions.

The first one stops me. Who am I and who am I looking for?

Lesbian, seeking a woman?

Straight, seeking a man?

Bi, seeking animal/vegetable/mineral?

Generally I prefer women. Generally I find them softer, silkier, stronger-hearted. But for me, right now, women are too close to the fire. My heart is still covered with third-degree woman-burns. Also, it's hard to imagine a sizable pool of sixtysomething lesbians who are kind enough to be gentle with me and adventurous enough to be into recreational sex. So I list myself as a bisexual woman who's seeking a man for "short-term dating" or "casual sex."

This brings me to profile question two. My age.

I'd planned to include "honest" on my list of winning traits. "What you see is what you get." "Self-aware and direct." "No games, except the fun kind." "Photos are current." Like that. But when a woman is looking for a little reparative nooky, could there be a less sexy number than sixty-two? It's no big deal to shave off a couple of years, is it? Anyway, everyone says I look younger than I am. Anyway, I can keep up with any actual fiftysomething, male or female.

Anyway, according to my research—a five-minute shallow dive into a 2010 OKCupid study fittingly called "The Big Lies People Tell in Online Dating"— everyone lies about everything on these sites. Men add two inches (to their height, that is; the study doesn't mention more intimate measurements). Women add an inch of height and deduct pounds from their weight. Both genders add 20 percent or more to their incomes. Two-thirds of profile photos are three or more years old. Also, apparently I'm not the only bisexual of the opportunist variety: 75 percent of bisexuals are fronting, actually dating only one gender. "Like bi men," the report concludes, "most bi women are, for whatever reason, not observably bi. The primacy of America's most popular threesome, two dudes and an Xbox, is safe."

With a few keystrokes, I transform myself into a fifty-eight-year-old. Approximately three seconds after I hit save, my e-mail inbox lights up like an amygdala mainlining dopamine.

Hello pretty how are you doing today and am billy by name what about you?

How are you doing today sweet Damsel?

Hi dear, good evening and how r u doing. like your profile n will like to get close n know more about u.

Hello beautiful, I just joined some mins ago . . . I must confess that your profile really caught my attention, and i must say you are beautiful

Wow, what a beauty you are, i never come across a beauty before were your parents a Greek god because it takes two gods to make a goddess like you, are you single?

hello dear nice to ready from you am so happy to hear this from you this my phone number (xxx) xxx-xxxx. just to make a good friend to each other so that we can be text each other or to call each other ok. or can i have your e-mail so that we can have a nice chat to each other time to time. bcos am a widow man and looking for a loyal woman to chat with to make me happy and i will also make you happy as well. best regard Michael smith

Just as I'm realizing why my therapist warned me that I might find the online dating world more injurious than curative, a different kind of message catches my eye.

I'm a writer too; based in Malibu but otherwise stunned by our statistical compatibility. I would very much like to test the algorithm that has paired us like chocolate and peanut butter, Champagne and rose petals, Kavalier & Clay. Hope you find that an interesting proposition. Thomas

A semicolon, a capital C for Champagne, intelligent flirting, *and* a literary reference, all in one message? How can I resist? I write back. Thomas writes back, a bit more cleverly. I write back, more cleverly still. We're writers, after all, jazz riffing from the West Side to the East. I check Thomas's profile page. His photos aren't bad. He says he's fifty-five, and he actually looks it.

As our online conversation continues over the next few days, I start to feel hopeful. With a woman this might come to nothing sexier than a cup of chamomile tea in a Wi-Fi café. But this is a man I'm jousting with. Last time I checked—admittedly, a couple of decades ago—when it comes to the pursuit of sex, men don't fuck around.

Thomas invites me to join him for dinner on Friday night at Lucques, a West Hollywood hot spot with a James Beard–winning chef and eyebrow-raising prices. I call Hannah, my longest happily married heterosexual friend, for a consult.

"I haven't slept with a man in twenty years," I tell her. "Anything I need to know?"

"Lingerie," Hannah says. "They love that. The tackier, the better."

"Check. I have exactly one set of matching red lace undies. From Ross Dress for Less. Anything else?"

"Condoms. Promise me you'll use condoms."

"God, men are a pain. But okay, I promise."

"Speaking of pain, if you're seeing him this weekend, you'd better get started on your hormone cream now. It takes a few days to work."

"You mean lube?"

"No, darling," Hannah says. "Estrogen cream. So you can get that thing of his into that thing of yours without feeling like you're being ripped open with a knife."

"*What?*"

Hannah sighs. "Welcome to postmenopausal heterosexuality. Every time Michael and I want to have sex, we have to decide days ahead of time, so I can get my body ready and he can get his little blue pills. It's like planning a military operation. I'd give sex up entirely, but he loves it. And I love him. So I do what makes him happy."

Jesus. Hannah's a brilliant, successful, powerful sixty-four-year-old woman. And she doesn't like sex? And she does it anyway?

"You're lucky. You have the option of skipping the whole mess and sticking with women," Hannah suggests. "That's what I'd do if I were you."

"I'd love to," I say, "if I could find a woman to do it with."

"You could, if you were willing to wait," Hannah points out.

Of course she's right. And of course I'm not willing to wait. For one thing, I never have been, and it seems a little late to start now.

For another thing, I need a distraction from a growing sense of unease about my job. I've been getting a weird vibe from Isabel lately—nothing I can name, and therefore nothing I can do anything about, just a sense of impending trouble.

WHEN I ARRIVE at ivy-draped Lucques, Thomas is seated at the best booth in the house, his evenly planed face lit by the fireplace's glow. He stands to greet me, kisses me on one cheek, then the other. He smells good. Okay, so he's a couple of inches shorter than his stated height. But his face is actually more handsome in person, his body tight and trim, his V-neck sweater cashmere, his shoes elegant yet hip.

Over $19 cocktails Thomas lavishes me with compliments about my outfit, my wit, my hair. His flattery is a bit effusive, but undeniably pleasant, appropriate for the task at hand.

Thomas asks me attentive questions, listens attentively to my answers. The chef comes to our table, sets down two tiny plates of caviar amuses-bouches. Thomas stands and they hug. Am I imagining it, or is Thomas sneaking peeks at me to make sure I'm suitably impressed?

Over diver scallops crudo with yellow tomato gazpacho, Thomas moves to my side of the booth, positions himself so our thighs are pressed against each other's. I guess I'm not a bi-impersonator after all. I feel the forces of lust gathering not far from where his leg brushes mine.

Over hanger steak with cannellini bean panzanella, Thomas takes my hand, traces lazy, sexy circles in my palm with one finger. Oh my God, I think. This is actually going to happen. Is this desire I'm feeling, or panic? Or both?

Over a shared corn ice cream sundae with cornmeal blondies and salted toffee sauce, Thomas asks me to follow him to his Malibu beach house to have sex with his wife while he watches. "Or," he offers, "you can leave your car here and spend the night with us, and I'll bring you back in the morning."

Oh.

Oh.

"If I pass on your offer," I say, "can I still eat my half of the sundae?"

Thomas looks confused. Then he laughs. "Of course," he says. "But I wish you'd reconsider."

"Not going to happen," I say, spooning hot, salty caramel sauce into my mouth.

The valet, plus tip, costs more than I would have spent if I'd stayed home and ordered takeout. I guess Thomas would have covered that if I'd said yes. Compared to the emotional fallout of that, the twenty bucks seems like a steal.

I'M TEMPTED TO GIVE UP on dating for another year or another decade, but that won't get me across the bridge. Out there in my world of writers, artists, and sixties refugees, there's got to be one man or one woman who wants to take a no-strings, tender tumble with me. I e-mail a few friends who know me well enough not to ask what I'm looking for or why I'm looking for it.

A New York painter writes to e-introduce me to her studio-mate, Maya, a fifty-year-old Brooklyn art professor and single lesbian who's headed to L.A. to interview for a job. Over e-mail, then a few phone calls, Maya and I establish a jokey, flirtatious connection. When I first see her on my FaceTime screen, I think, "I could totally lie down with this woman."

But can I do that and then get up again, without hurting her or myself? Maya seems to be just what the love doctor ordered: pretty and upbeat, animated and sweet. On the other hand, she's a fifty-year-old woman. I haven't met many of those who check the "casual sex" box without mentally checking "by which I mean long-term relationship."

"You're like some horrible horny frat boy," Celia tells me.

"What's wrong with sex sans attachment? As long as I'm honest."

"That's what all the horrible horny frat boys say."

During our last phone call before Maya leaves for L.A., I tell her exactly what I'm ready for and not ready for and why. I tell her that my bungalow is my safety zone, off-limits to strangers, even strangers with whom I'm planning a hot tryst. I tell her that if my frat-boy approach is a deal-breaker, I'll understand.

Maya asks why I'm repeating myself. She says I was clear from the start. She assures me that she isn't in the market for a girl-friend and that she's always up for some fun. "How cool it is that we found each other," she says cheerily, "so we can share a few days of that?" Hugely relieved, hugely nervous, hugely excited, I arrange to spend a long weekend in Maya's hotel room on Her-mosa Beach.

"Do you want my AARP membership number?" I ask. "I can probably get you a discount."

"Oh, definitely," Maya says with distinct sarcasm. "I'll call up this totally straight hotel in this totally straight beach town and tell them the woman who's coming to my room for hot sex is a senior citizen, and we want the AARP discount."

I laugh. Three thousand miles and ten years away, Maya laughs. And then we're laughing so hard I have a tiny pee-leakage incident, befitting the senior citizen I am.

I HAVEN'T BEEN NAKED in front of a new lover since 1996, and my body has sustained some serious damage since then. With just twenty-four hours to make myself tryst-ready, I text Charlotte, my L.A. style guru, to ask where she gets waxed. Her salon of choice is called, enticingly, Paradise Spa.

"It's not fancy, but they do a great job," Charlotte says. "And it's cheap." Better yet, Paradise is conveniently located a few blocks from Bellissima. Things are still strange at work, which makes me nervous about leaving for an hour, even at lunchtime. But a girl has to do what a girl has to do.

My first surprise, upon entering the pearlescent gates of Paradise, is delivered by an aesthetician who introduces herself, through a thick Korean accent, as Candy. Candy grabs my elbow and steers me into a wax-splattered cubicle, yanks the pale-blue curtain closed, and makes the universal hand signal for "Get naked." In Berkeley, the waxing women worked around my panties, enlisting my hands to make the relevant crevices available, taking great care to keep their own fingers at a respectable distance from my erogenous zones.

Not so Paradise. Factory-farmed chickens are plucked more gently than this. Waxing always hurts, but this hurts more. I bite my lips to keep from yowling as Candy dips and rips, rips and dips, grunting gutturally with each jerk of a paper strip as if she's setting fire to *her* mons pubis, not mine.

Then Candy barks something at me that sounds like "Gamm robot."

I regard her uncomprehendingly. She repeats the unintelligible phrase.

I give Candy the universal shrug for "Huh?" Candy gives me the universal hand signal for "Flip over." Like Helen Keller at the water fountain, I suddenly understand that she's been saying "Give me your butt."

No Berkeley aesthetician ever asked for my butt. Nor would I have given it to her. But I'm a stranger in a strange land, doing what the Romans do. I have no idea what Candy has in mind for my butt, but whatever it is, she does it all day every day. What could possibly go wrong?

"Best offer I've had in years," I mutter, and flip onto my belly.

This time I *do* yell out loud. There's no helping it. Candy is tearing the skin off my netherest region.

"Too much hair," she says. I sit up, wincing, to find Candy shaking her head disapprovingly. "Come sooner next time," she says. I don't bother to explain that she's just gone where no waxer has ever been.

I stagger out of Paradise and back to work, my inner thighs Velcroed to each other by sticky residue. In the Bellissima bathroom I take a deep breath, step in front of the mirror, and face the newly truly naked me.

Nothing in decades of Berkeley bikini waxing prepared me for this. I see more of myself than I've seen since age eleven. In fact, that's exactly how my pudendum looks: like it belongs to an eleven-year-old. Is this what Joanne had in mind for me? Making myself attractive to lovers who want sex with preadolescent girls?

I'm meeting Maya in five hours. I'm not sure what to hope for at this point. Growing my pubic hair back by tonight doesn't seem possible. A merkin, though no doubt available at any of the many prop houses within blocks of here, seems like a tacky accessory to wear to a first date. Hoping that Maya doesn't have pedophile predilections, I pray that I'm not her first Brazilian'ed lover.

———

MY HEART IS POUNDING, my armpits damp with dread as I pull open the seawater-spattered glass door of the Whaler's Inn. I look around the lobby and there she is, my late-life deflowerer, smiling at me from a navy blue easy chair, her unlined face lit by an anchor-shaped lamp. She stands to greet me. As Maya's photos promised, she's a few inches taller than I am, with a leaner, stronger body than mine.

Damn. She's ten years younger *and* better looking? How am I supposed to summon a shred of confidence? Looking at her makes me want to keep my clothes on. Knowing what we're here for makes me want to take them off.

Am I really going to do this? Have sex with a stranger?

Maya pulls me close, runs her hands down my back. I feel her breasts against my breasts, her hipbones against mine. I feel like lying down with her this minute in this cheesy lobby. I feel like throwing up.

"We fit," Maya murmurs into my ear.

I nod against her shoulder awkwardly. I'm a pimply-faced fourteen-year-old boy.

"You feel good," Maya whispers. "Let's go upstairs."

"Did you—" I stammer, gesturing at the reception desk.

"I checked us in." Maya takes a step back and smiles at me. "Old-farts' discount and all."

She takes my hand and leads me to the elevator. The moment the elevator door closes behind us, she does what she'd promised to do, what I'd asked her to do, to keep me from changing my mind. She gives me no choice. She presses me against the wall and she pushes into me and she grabs my hair and she kisses me hard.

I don't feel it.

No. That's not it.

I feel it. But I don't want it.

The elevator glides to a stop. I follow Maya down the carpeted hall, past pastel prints of sailboats and pelicans.

"This is us," she says. She opens the door, pulls me inside. She puts her hands on my shoulders, looks into my eyes. "You sure you're good with this?" she asks me.

"Positive," I lie.

"I want you. Do you want me?"

I nod, and she kisses me again. I close my eyes. I don't like what I see inside my head, so I open them again. Kissing Maya feels nothing like kissing my wife. Beyond her shoulders a king-sized percale island awaits us. I tell myself I'll like this more when we're actually in bed.

"I love your dress," Maya murmurs, pulling it over my head. She lays me back against the pile of pillows, wriggling out of her shearling vest, her shocking pink minidress. "I love *this*," she says hoarsely, running her hands down my sides.

I burst into tears. And suddenly I'm sobbing from the deepest place in me, crying and coughing and gulping for air, and I can't stop.

Maya wraps us both in the bedspread, holds me like a swaddled child. "It's okay," she says. "Go ahead. Cry."

Maya holds me until the room is dark and I'm catching my breath, hiccupping and dripping snot. "Sexy," I say, reaching for a Kleenex. "Sorry."

"Don't be sorry. You're fine. Don't go anywhere." She pads into the bathroom. I feel better without her. And I want her to come back.

I hear water running. Oh, good, I think: she's taking a shower. She'll be gone for a while. I take a deep breath, let it out. But then she's back, carrying a white terry-cloth robe.

"I'm running us a bath," Maya says, wrapping me in the robe. It's heavy and soft and warm. How could I have imagined going back to men? Women are everything. Hot lover, compassionate friend, nurturing mom.

"I thought I was ready," I say, blowing my nose, elephant style. "If I'd known, I wouldn't have—"

Maya touches a manicured, calloused finger to my lips. "Let's take a bath," she says, pulling me off the bed.

I don't want to take a bath with Maya. I want to go home. But how can I say no to this sweet woman?

Maya leads me into the bathroom. I let her take off my robe. She climbs into the tub and beckons to me. I lean back against her tight torso and soft breasts and I look at our legs splayed out in front of us, hers long and muscular and pale, mine thicker and tanned.

I turn around and for the first time I look at Maya, really look at her. She looks nothing like my wife. And she looks really good.

"Can I kiss you?" I say.

Maya does what I ask her to do, the things my wife didn't need me to ask her to do. She does things she wants to do, things I don't know to ask her to do. It feels good and it makes me cry and it feels good and it makes me cry and it makes me cry and it feels good. I start to lose myself, I start to go, and then I see my wife's face floating behind my closed eyes, and my eyes fly open.

"Sorry," I pant. "I just can't."

Maya rolls over me and lies next to me and takes me into her arms.

In the morning the room is daytime bright despite the closed blackout drapes. Is there no way to get a break from the goddamn sunshine of L.A.?

Across the tangled white expanse, a stranger sleeps. A pretty stranger who picked me up and walked me across that bridge, who gave me pleasure and received it. No one could have been kinder than Maya was to me last night. No one could have moved more smoothly between nurturing and seduction, between passion and care.

Maya stretches, purrs, opens her eyes and smiles. "Morning," she says, reaching for me.

I don't want to touch her. I want to jump up, throw on my clothes, and go home.

But I climb into Maya's arms and I give that walk across the bridge another try.

When I leave the Whaler's Inn on Sunday night, it's done. My wife is no longer the last person I'll ever have sex with, even if I'm pretty sure she's still the last person I'll ever love.

FIFTEEN

I n my old life, my married life, I was the world's worst hostess. I was fine with cohosting the dinner parties and backyard barbecues and Christmas-Eve-oysters-and-Champagne feasts that my wife and I threw. When a guest had too many oysters or too much fun, I was fine with tucking her into our pristine, underutilized guest bed. For one night.

A two-nighter? Doable.

Three nights? Teeth-grittable.

But when friends without hotel budgets—which is to say, our friends—asked to stay longer than a weekend, I'd instantly shed my identity as a perpetually oversharing memoirist and become a member of that heretofore mysterious species, the "private person." The threat of a long-term guest, especially from my wife's side of the aisle, turned me into the Locked-Nest Monster, imagining my foibles and farts and fakeries exposed; my pathetic finances stretched beyond the breaking point, my daily doings observed.

As it happened, I shared my fortress with a far more generous soul. My wife hosted her friends and mine with grace and enthusiasm, which made her foe, not friend, when it came to repelling interlopers. Each time a guest threatened a stay, I attempted to recruit my wife to the cause. *I have a book to finish. You know I can't write with people in the house. Easy for you to be welcoming—you're never home. I'm having a root canal that week; I need solitude when I'm in pain.*

When my efforts failed, I was not above sidling up to my wife, nuzzling her neck, and asking her how I could possibly make loud, beautiful love to her with a houseguest in the next room.

The truth, dim to me then but blazingly obvious now: I was a possessive, insecure, developmentally arrested child posing as an adult; a cheapskate with a scarcity mentality and a balance sheet tattooed onto my brain. I saw houseguests as freeloaders who were out to drain me emotionally and financially. I was an Olympic-level control freak who wanted my life and my wife to myself.

I knew better. Of course I did. I was an early adopter of the sharing economy. I came of age in communes, for Christ's sake. I'd been in therapy since the age of five. I was aware of my abandonment issues and trust issues; I'd paid good money to learn the importance of not inflicting them on others. I knew I *should* openheartedly offer shelter to those who needed it, just as many people, over the decades, had openheartedly offered shelter to me.

I wanted to keep my out-of-town friends. I wanted my wife to keep hers—the ones I liked, at least. I wanted to stay married. And so, having failed to enlist my wife in my campaign, I'd gulp down dread and preemptive annoyance and squeak out the requisite invitation.

Intentions be damned. I just couldn't pull it off. Arrival day invariably proved that my mouth had written a check my soul couldn't cash. Feeling trapped and resentful, I'd "welcome" our guests with a forced smile and an icy hug. Then I'd spend the duration of their visits secretly listing the interloper's atrocities: doors left open or closed too loudly, empty coffee cups left on nightstands for whole minutes at a time, my fancy toothpaste wantonly consumed. As I counted down the days till departure, my grievances swarmed like tsetse flies in my cold black heart. Even if I'd liked our guests before they arrived, by the time they left I hated them for "making" me feel and behave so meanly. I knew I was right about them, whether my wife saw it or not. Out of love for her, I felt it was my responsibility to point out her friends' flaws. "You deserve to be treated better than this," I'd advise her, sidestepping the fact that I was the one who was treating her badly. "Your friends are taking advantage of you."

I saw my case as airtight the night I came home to find Stacy, a Chicago friend of my wife's, sitting at our kitchen table, staring into space with an empty bottle of expensive vodka in front of her. Our expensive vodka, of course.

"Are you okay?" I asked Stacy, concealing my resentment under a veneer of faux concern. Stacy cast her bloodshot eyes in my general direction and nodded wobbily. "I finished off your booze. Sorry about that."

"No problem," I said, and went to bed to lie in wait for my wife.

"Did you talk to Stacy?" I whispered when my wife got into bed, certain we were about to resolve our houseguest problem once and for all.

I felt my wife's body tense up. "Uh-huh. Why?"

"She's drunk."

"So?"

"On our vodka."

"So?"

A million responses flew to my lips, all of them useless. There was nothing I could say to convince my wife to stop inviting these moochers to our house or, better yet, to drop them entirely. After a few years, they simply stopped showing up. Did I kvetch in my sleep? Or did the straight white line of my mouth tell them all they needed to know?

I knew I was hurting my friends, my wife, my marriage, myself. My wife and I should have talked about it—fought about it, probably—but that would have broken our unspoken peace-at-all-costs rule. Instead of asking me what it would take to make me a happy—happier, at least—hostess to her friends, my wife glared at me and went out drinking with them. Instead of apologizing to my wife for my awful behavior, which might have forced me to actually change it, I made like a cheating husband and kissed up to her till she forgave me. Or seemed to.

Maybe if my wife had pitched a fit or I'd woman'd up and grown up, we'd still be married. But she didn't and I didn't, and we're not. And so now I'm living in a room of my own for the first time in my sixty-two years, without parents, boyfriend, husband, kids, girlfriend, or wife—but with a guest studio of my own. I won't know if that's a denial-driven setup for disaster or an opportunity for redemption until someone asks to use it.

It's bound to happen soon. At sixty-two I have a striped past: lots of "geographics" pulled and therefore, lots of friends in lots of places. Now I live in a city that many people—writers and artists, especially—have reason to visit. As Hannah told me soon after my move to L.A., when I was worrying about staying connected to my Bay Area friends, "Everyone comes to L.A. eventually. Just sit here and wait. They'll all show up."

The past two years proved Hannah correct. Even when I was renting my itsy-bitsy apartment with only my couch to offer, I entertained a steady stream of visitors from the East Coast, the Bay Area, and places in between. My friends were happy to have an L.A. place to crash, and—miracle of miracles—I was happy to host them.

SURE ENOUGH, a few weeks after I move into the Bungalito, a Brooklyn friend, Dana, e-mails to ask if she can stay with me while she writes a TV pilot based on her novel. Proposed duration of her visit: six weeks.

Instead of filling me with dread, Dana's e-mail thrills me. I've adored Dana since we met at an artists' colony ten years ago. We bonded instantly, went halfies on a blender and an industrial-size bottle of tequila, and spent a month of evenings drinking margaritas in her studio, telling each other everything. Dana never made it to the Bay Area, but I see her whenever I go to New York, which isn't nearly often enough. For some margarita-related reason neither of us remembers, Dana and I call each other Chiquita or, in extra-affectionate moments, Chica.

"Come for as long as you can stay," I write back, noting how good it feels good to say that and mean it.

———

WHEN DANA and her multiple suitcases appear at my front door, I'm a bit trepidatious, willing the Monster not to breathe fire on her. But no. I'm thrilled to see her. We take the five-minute, four-room Bungalito tour. "A writing balcony!" Dana says. "So much light!"

Dana follows me down the stairs to the deck. "Wow," she says. "Look at that garden. You have a *fountain*!"

I open the French doors to the casita. Dana and I step inside.

"It's fantastic, Chiquita." Dana sinks into a chair at the kitchen table and regards me thoughtfully. "Last time I saw you, your whole life was falling apart. And now look at what you've created. I'm so impressed."

I'm getting used to people coming here and saying that. But it never fails to make me teary grateful.

"If you could do this . . ." Dana's voice trails off. We sit in silence for a moment. Past experience with visiting friends tells me what Dana's about to say, and she says it. "It makes me wonder what *I* could do. What I *should* do."

"Are you kidding?" I argue. "HBO bought your *novel*! And they're paying you to turn it into a screenplay. I'd *kill* for that to happen to me."

"I'm living in a gigantic house full of all kinds of pre-divorce crap I don't even want. Not because I like it. Just because of inertia."

"Inertia's a powerful thing."

"Do you ever miss your stuff?" Dana asks me.

"Not really."

"Amazing. God, I'd love to live in a cozy little place like this."

"With two kids?"

"You know what I mean."

"Yeah. I do." But being envied, especially by someone as accomplished as Dana, feels weird. "Wine?"

Dana nods and we traipse back upstairs to my kitchen. "What smells so good?" she asks.

I lift the lid on the pot that's simmering on the stove. "Pot roast. For our dinner tonight." I beam at Dana, anticipating her delight and her praise. No more Locked-Nest Monster. Who could be a more mostest hostess than I?

"That's so sweet of you," Dana says. "But I made dinner plans for tonight. Sorry, Chica. I didn't know . . ."

"No prob," I say around a mouthful of disappointment. "We'll have dinner another time."

"Tomorrow night?"

"You don't have to commit," I say. "I know you're going to be super busy while you're here."

"Chiquita! You're being weird! I *want* to have dinner with you."

I glance at Dana. She looks sincere, not pitying. "Okay," I say. "The pot roast will be better tomorrow, anyway."

"I'm going to get some great work done here. I can feel it." Dana grabs me and hugs me. "Thanks for understanding. You're the best."

Not the best, I think. But getting better.

HOSTING A FELLOW NEW YORKER, showing her the secret corners of L.A. that my friends have shown me, makes me fall even more in love with this town. And that's how it feels: like a passionate romance. It's not just my brain that reacts when I'm driving east on the 101 and the Hollywood skyline comes into view. My *body* reacts to the sight of the thirteen-story Capitol Records Building, where Frank Sinatra and the Beach Boys recorded on vinyl. The giant neon Patrón tequila bottle that lights the streets of Hollywood at night. The Roosevelt Hotel, built by Douglas Fairbanks, Mary Pickford, and Louis B. Mayer; home to the first Academy Awards in 1929; crash pad for Clark Gable, Carole Lombard, and my girl, Marilyn Monroe.

Same when I'm driving north on PCH and the Pacific comes into view, dotted with bobbing surfers and seals and, sometimes, porpoises and whales. Same when I hike up to the Griffith Observatory and lean over the railing like a tourist, captivated by the Hollywood sign. Same when I'm taking Melrose home and I glimpse the neon Western Exterminator sign that was my beacon when I was new in town, relentlessly disoriented, as dependent on my iPhone as my babies were on my breasts.

Forget Texas. Everything's big in L.A., where "flea market" means the Rose Bowl Flea Market, 2,500 booths full of lamps and jewelry and martini shakers that might have belonged to Cary Grant or—who knows?—Marilyn Monroe.

The Hollywood Farmers' Market means a year-round hundred-ring circus, where every species of fruit and vegetable and flower is offered, every hue of green juice is pressed, every genre of street musician plays while the children of rock stars and movie stars and ordinary people squint into the sunshine, petting baby goats and having their faces painted while their parents navigate the throng, their famous faces quasi-hidden by huge wildflower bouquets.

The meaning of "going to the movies" depends on the time of

year and, as in all things L.A., the amount of money one is prepared to pay for the level of experience one can afford to have. In this industry town, where the home screening room is as common in certain zip codes as the microwave is in others, luxury multiplexes are furnished with real leather recliners, and guests are served icy martinis and steak frites and local artisan hot fudge sundaes in their cushy seats.

Between November and February, the question "How can you tell when it's winter in L.A.?" is answerable in two words: awards season. At Christmastime, instead of snow and tinsel, L.A. is blanketed by free DVDs of the current year's TV shows and films. Studios seeking nominations send out thousands of their top contenders for the Screen Actors' Guild Awards, the Emmys, the Golden Globes, and the brass ring, the Oscars. During my first winter in L.A., I was telling a friend about a movie I'd just seen at my local theater. "You *paid* to see a movie during *awards season*?" she howled.

How can I be so besotted by a city? Journalist Melody Warnick wrote a book on the subject: *This Is Where You Belong: The Art and Science of Loving the Place You Live.*

"People are on a search to find their place the same way they're on a search to find a partner or spouse," Warnick writes, quoting place consultant Katherine Loflin.

"Feeling connected, engaged, a little bit in love with our city? That's the kind of place attachment whose effects . . . [make us] less anxious, less likely to suffer heart attacks or strokes, and less likely to complain about ailments.

"In a study conducted in Tokyo," Warnick writes, "elderly Japanese women who were attached to [their neighborhoods] were more likely to be alive five years down the road than women who didn't care one way or the other."

Warnick includes a place attachment scale developed by researchers—a series of statements used to gauge respondents' connection to where they live. I take the quiz, and my agreement with statements like "I feel like I belong in this community," "If I could live anywhere in the world, I would live here," and "The people who live here are my kind of people" tells me what I already know: at least geographically, I'm happy where I am.

This Is Where You Belong opens with a quote from Joan Didion, a formerly ambivalent Angeleno. "A place belongs forever to whoever claims it hardest, wrenches it from itself, shapes it, renders it, loves it so radically that he remakes it in its own image."

I don't know how much I've shaped Los Angeles or remade it in my own image, but the opposite is definitely true. I belong to Los Angeles because it has claimed me hard, wrenched me out of myself, shaped me. All the lucky breaks I've had since I came to L.A. make me feel that the city loves me so radically that it has, at least partially, remade me in its own sunshiny image.

I feel *matched* by this showy, kaleidoscopic, overblown, electric, drama-queen city. Like L.A., I've been so down it looked like up to me. Like L.A., I'm making a comeback. Like L.A., I am at once old and new. Joni Mitchell asked L.A. to "take me as I am," and L.A. is saying to me what it said to her: Bring it, baby. Bring it all.

Since New York, I've never been surrounded by so many people like me, so many of the kinds of people I like: writers, artists, bohos, leftists, hikers, style freaks, foodies, bigmouths, world travelers, self-reinventors, and, it must be said, Jews.

Two years in, I've gathered a small but sturdy stable of truly trustable friends. When I need a place to sleep because I'm lonely, or a place to write where the chores staring at me aren't mine, I spend a weekend in Santa Monica at Hannah and Michael's. For Thanksgiving feasts, New Year's Day black-eyed peas, July Fourth barbecues, or emotional emergencies, I always have a home and a cocktail waiting at Donna and Nichole's. For little-kid-time, I have options: a pool party with Charlotte and Brian's spunky boys, or a game of "Name That Mammal" at the dinner table with Darcy, Bruce, and their bright-eyed eight-year-old, Zakiyah. Every Sunday morning I walk into a room full of fellow Al-Anon members, many of whose names I don't know, but whose presence in the same seat, week after week, makes me feel like there is some sort of order in my world.

Every few nights, Dana knocks on my kitchen door with a bottle of wine and a bar of dark Belgian chocolate. I light the candles and we sit at my table and eat my food and drink her wine and we talk and talk about our books, her script, our aging bodies, my new friends, our mutual friends, our mutual friends' books, the fifteen pounds we've both wanted to lose since we were teenagers, our breakups, our love lives and lack thereof.

I watch Dana's flashing blue eyes as she talks, and I listen to the fascinating things she has to say about what happened today in the writers' room on the Paramount lot, and my chest feels like a balloon inflated to bursting, and I think, This is actually my life now.

There's a trick to giving, and I'm getting it. I'm getting that Dana was put on this earth to be Dana, not to make up for everything and everyone I've ever wanted and do not have. The wonders of Dana, the deficits of Dana, the way being with her makes me feel smart and loving and alive, the way being with her makes me feel needy and desperate: I get to choose which of my feelings to pay attention to. And I get to choose which parts to discuss with Dana (the good stuff) and which parts to wrestle with on my own or with my therapist or sponsor (the rest).

Halfway through Dana's stay, Hannah and I invite a dozen of our L.A. writer friends to a brunch for Dana at Hannah's grown-up Westside house. We sit around Hannah's long dinner table drinking mimosas and eating Hannah's homemade quiche and talking about character development and whose book is on the *New York Times* bestseller list and why no one can live on a writer's income anymore and how Obamacare and Airbnb might help.

And while I'm eating and drinking and arguing and laughing, I'm also asking myself: what's not to love about this life?

PART THREE

HALF-FULL

SIXTEEN

My Plan B life feels a lot like Plan A, except for one thing. I'm still single. And I'd still prefer not to be. After my last foray into the dating fray, I'm hesitant to dive back in. But that singleness isn't going to fix itself.

I pull up some dating sites, contemplate the pages and pages of questions. I should be good at this. I've been writing marketing copy since I could hold a pen. My Don Draper dad had my brother and me naming sodas at the dinner table, brainstorming Pepsi taglines in the car. Decades later, between book deals, I farmed myself out to various socially responsible businesses, writing ads and newsletters and catalogue copy to pay the bills.

If I can sell Mountain Dew to Pepsi drinkers and Ben & Jerry's politics to its shareholders and Bellissima's hemp dresses to its eco-demographic, surely I can sell myself to that one brilliant, beautiful, gregarious, witty, left-leaning, adventurous, curious, outdoorsy, upbeat but not chirpy, deep but not morose, well-traveled, book-reading, stylish but not superficial lesbian who lives within twenty miles of me.

Browsing the thumbnail shots of my "matches" is not encouraging. A theme emerges, and it is not encouraging, either: women French-kissing their dogs. How is this anyone's idea of seduction? Also, when did lesbians get dogs? While I was happily married through the nineties and 00s, what happened to lesbians and cats?

Subthemes reveal themselves. Big women posing on big motorcycles. Heavily made-up women slugging drinks in bars. Butches seeking femmes, Christians seeking Christians, straight married women plagued by bi-curiosity.

One woman stands out from the rest. She's pretty, and the smile in her eyes has a distinct spark of irony. Unlike all the others', her profile shot is black-and-white, but the buttons on her shirt are turquoise, the only spots of color in the shot.

I click the heart icon next to her picture and send her a message: "Are you black and white in person, or do you come (so to speak) in colors?—Meredith."

Five seconds later, her answer: "Meredith . . . why don't you see for yourself? Call me and we'll find a slice of time to say hi. Helena."

Procrastinating won't help. I take a deep breath and dial her number.

"I like your pace," Helena answers.

"I like your buttons," I say.

We fall into an awkward silence, which I attempt to fill by asking the crucial Los Angeles relationship-potential question. "I live in Silver Lake. What about you?"

"Sherman Oaks," Helena says.

I've never heard of Sherman Oaks. But my craigslist purchasing has introduced me to dozens of cities I'd never heard of, all of which proved to be within dating proximity of L.A. "How far is that?" I ask.

"Fifteen minutes from Beverly Hills at seven on Sunday mornings. An hour and a half during rush hour. I grew up here, so I'm used to spending my life in my car."

"What do you do in Beverly Hills at seven on Sunday mornings?" Please God, I pray silently, don't let it be church.

"SoulCycle. I ride five or six times a week. It's my spinogogue."

I laugh, and Helena laughs, and then we're talking and laughing and it's good. It's not an instant cosmic connection, but by the time Helena and I hang up, we're teasing each other with the familiarity of old friends, and we've made a dinner date for Friday night. Helena says she'll pick the place and book a table and get back to me.

I like the way Helena takes charge. I allow myself to imagine having a competent partner again, to sit in the passenger seat every now and then. How nice it would be to be treated to a meal or an Uber ride, to be a tiny bit spoiled, a tiny bit taken care of.

I know when I need some adult supervision. I call Celia and get her voice mail. Hannah, as usual, answers on the first ring. "You're futurizing," she says, a favorite word of hers. "Stay in the present. Just go out with her and see how you feel."

"Clearly the way I feel is not to be trusted," I say.

"That's because you're dating with a broken heart. Kudos for getting out there. But you're bound to have a negative reaction to meeting someone."

"You think it's too soon?"

Hannah sighs. "Why don't you have dinner with this person? All will be revealed in good time."

"Right," I say, and start planning my outfit. Am I going for sophisticated? Sexy? Thrift-store high-end designer, or thrift-store boho? Who do I want this Helena person to think I am? Who do I want to be?

PULLING UP to a West Hollywood hot spot called Laurel Hardware, I feel expansive and fancy, in the flow of La-La life. In that spirit, I decide to pay the twelve bucks to valet, denying WeHo the joy of towing my car for a third time. The hostess leads me to a woodsy, romantic patio lit by strands of white bulbs woven through delicate, boxed olive trees. At French wicker tables, twenty- and thirtysomething guys in porkpie hats with bushy beards and girls wearing spiked gladiator sandals sip cocktails and push food around their plates.

Helena is sitting straight-backed at the best table in the house, right in the center of the beatific, buzzing crowd. As she watches me approach, her face is composed, the full moon lighting her artfully streaked, shoulder-length hair. She looks a little older than she did in her pictures, but then, so do I. She stands as I approach the table. I love her height, which is five-ten, as advertised. Helena puts out her hand, as if this is a business meeting. We shake.

A young waitress with Amy Winehouse hair materializes tableside. "Hey, are you a rock star?" she asks Helena. I examine the girl's smooth face for irony. I find none. "You look like a rocker," she adds.

Helena seems pleased. "I just play one on TV."

The server squints at her.

"Kidding," Helena says. "Meredith, what would you like?"

So she *is* planning to pay. Thank goddess, girl-chivalry is not dead.

I order a Manhattan. Helena orders sparkling water. "We'll have the Brussels sprouts," Helena tells our server, "and a beet salad for the table." She puts the menu down. "We'll decide about the rest in a bit."

My Manhattan, paired with Helena's self-confidence, smooths my nervous edges, and soon the two of us are talking and laughing again. We order ribs and salmon and a bunch of side dishes. It's fun, ordering too much food. It reminds me of every restaurant meal I ever had with my dad. When I raise my eyebrows at the cavalcade of plates arriving at our table, Helena even says what my dad used to say. "You can take the leftovers home."

"Why do *I* get the leftovers?" I ask her.

"I don't eat them," she answers. "And I have a feeling you're the leftovers type."

Is that an anti-Semitic dig? I don't think so. I think Helena's perceptive. This date is going really well. I chug my second Manhattan, wondering when Helena will kiss me. It's kind of spoiling the fun, the wondering. I want to get it over with. I think of the scene in *Annie Hall* when Alvy Singer kisses Annie under a lamppost on their way to dinner, "So now we can digest our food." I order another Manhattan. And then I reach my hands across the table and I pull Helena's face to mine and I kiss her.

Helena jerks her head away. "We're in public," she says.

"So?"

"So I'm a private person."

"Are you saying that because we're women?" I ask, aware that I'm trying to provoke her, to distract us both from my embarrassment.

I consider apologizing. But then I'd be apologizing for what I want. And if there's one good thing about being my age and single and pre-heartbroken, it's not having to apologize for what I want.

Conversation resumes. Helena seems unrattled. My third Manhattan renders me incapable of being rattled. Helena grabs the check from our server before I can even make a purse-swipe. "Can I leave the tip, at least?" I ask.

"Absolutely not," Helena says.

"Well, thank you," I say, and in that moment I feel our dynamic forming. I'll be the starving artist, she'll be the bountiful businesswoman. She'll be the reasonable grown-up, I'll be the impetuous child. She'll be the kisser, if indeed there is to be kissing. I'll be the kissed, when she chooses to kiss me.

I follow Helena to the valet stand. Her ass looks great in her skinny jeans.

Under the light of the valet stand, Helena scrutinizes my face. "Are you okay to drive? I can get you an Uber, and you can pick up your car tomorrow."

"I'm fine," I say.

Helena shrugs, shaking her pretty head. "Your call. Give me your valet ticket."

She hands my ticket and hers to the valet guy, along with a ten-dollar bill. This woman is way above my pay grade, and I like it. She's got money, and she's got class.

Helena gives me a stiff, brief hug and slides behind the wheel of a late-model black Mercedes coupe. She doesn't leave until my car arrives and I'm safely tucked into the driver's seat.

Driving home, I decide that Helena will never call me again, thanks to my grabby move. At least the date was good practice.

My phone rings as I walk through my front door. "Just making sure you got home safely," Helena says.

More girl-chivalry! I like it. "I hope we can see each other again," I say. There's something about this woman that makes me feel safe and secure, and those are some feelings I've been really wanting to have.

"I'd like that," Helena says distantly. Despite her lack of enthusiasm, a few days later I call and invite her to be my plus one at a friend's book launch party at the ultra-posh West Hollywood Soho House.

"I'll go on one condition," Helena says. "Do you think you can behave yourself this time?"

Behave myself? If a man said that to me, I'd read him the feminist riot act. But coming from Helena's mouth, it sounds affectionate. Admiring, almost. And very adult.

"What's so bad about bad behavior?" I say. I'm going for flirty, but I hear myself sounding like an impish child instead.

"Three words," Helena answers. "D. U. I."

"I'll behave," I promise. Helena's ten years younger than I am, but she seems older. I like that.

I kind of hoped Helena would be at least a bit intimidated by the party—its exclusive venue, its guest list, the fact that I was invited to it. No such luck. She shows up at Soho House in her glossy black car wearing a tight black miniskirt and black high-heeled boots that make her a full head taller than I am. "I brought out the legs," she says, stating the obvious. As we enter the elegantly appointed room, she tells me, "Go do your networking. Don't worry about me. I know how to have fun at a party."

So she does. Helena circulates among the glitterati, ignoring the lavish spread (always my first stop and main attraction), refusing the proffered cocktails, chatting with household-name writers and publicists. Twice I check in with her to find a writer friend of mine in the process of telling Helena that I've recently had my heart broken, and that if Helena hurts me, she'll be run out of town, or worse. Smiling her confident smile, Helena tells one and then the other friend not to worry. "Your friend is in good hands. I promise." Hearing this sends a little shiver of delight through my heavily Spanxed body.

HELENA AND I text incessantly through the week. She's a little heavy on the emoticons and LOLs, but bantering with her is fun. And she's so *there*. I feel like I can make mistakes and she won't disappear. It seems unlikely that she's looking for a threesome or a quick fuck. Weeks go by, and she makes zero moves, and it starts to seem unlikely that she's looking for a twosome or any kind of fuck.

A bit more gently this time, I take matters into my own hands. I invite Helena to hike a trail near her house on Sunday, and use that excuse to invoke the L.A. Rule: geography trumps all. As we're slogging down the dusty path toward the trail head parking lot, I tell her that driving long distances gives me a backache, which is true, and I ask if I can spend the night at her place after our hike, to break up the one-hour trip, which is not true.

"Sure," Helena says with zero affect.

Gulp. So I've got myself a girl who doesn't respond well to sexual aggression *or* sexual subtext. That doesn't leave me many options. I'm scrambling to come up with a winning strategy as I follow Helena to her place, a midcentury ranch house, fronted by manicured ferns and a purple statice hedge, bright green grass, immaculate porch, spotless sidewalk, someone's suburban dream come true.

"We painted our front door red, too," I say, standing next to Helena on the porch, looking for common ground, nervously waiting for her to turn her key in the lock. "My wife and I, I mean," I add.

I regret my words as soon they leave my mouth. Saying "my wife" as I'm trying to take someone else to bed feels like spitting glass.

Helena doesn't seem to have heard me. She walks around the pitch-dark living room, opening drapes and shutters. The room is sparsely decorated, with velvet chairs and couches in interesting, vaguely vintage colors and shapes.

Helena carries my overnight bag into a small, dark bedroom. "Fresh towels," she says, pointing to a neatly stacked, fluffy pile on the brown bedspread. "Let me know if you need anything else."

WTF? "Um. Is this the guest room?" I ask her.

Helena nods.

"You want me to sleep in the guest room?"

For the first time, I see discomfort on Helena's face. "I thought you'd like to have your own space."

Helena is from Mars, I think. I'm from Venus. How is this ever going to work? "You think I drove to Sherman Oaks for *space?*"

"I was just being courteous," Helena says.

Courteous? Who even uses that word? What does that word even *mean?*

Helena and I stare at each other across the miles of sky between our respective planets.

"I guess I misunderstood." I pick up my overnight bag.

"Don't be such a drama queen." Helena takes my bag out of my hands and beckons me to follow her to her bedroom. Outside the windows is a kidney-shaped swimming pool surrounded by a neat row of bird-of-paradise, their orange-and-purple faces leering at the turquoise tile. Helena sits on the edge of the king-sized bed and pats the Frette duvet cover next to her. "Okay, then. Come here."

Fortunately, sex with Helena is less traumatic than sex with Maya was. Unfortunately, sex with Helena isn't very . . . sexy. First time is never the best, I tell myself. And she's beautiful, with baby-soft skin.

Helena falls asleep curled around me, her arm across my chest. As the hours tick by, I lie on my back with my eyes wide open and my heart pounding, waiting for dawn, trying to will an Ambien out of my bag and into my mouth. Finally the room lightens; the sky turns the swimming pool pink. Helena sits up and pulls on the T-shirt I pulled off her last night. "Coffee? Tea?" she says.

"Tea, please," I say.

I hear a kettle whistling and I smell bread toasting and then Helena appears in the doorway in her Rag & Bone T-shirt and her long legs and nothing else, carrying two plates of scrambled eggs and avocado toast and a mug of Earl Grey tea. She hands me my plate and settles into bed next to me.

Staring down at my plate, I realize that, with rare exceptions, no lover has ever brought me breakfast in bed. Not my boyfriends, not my husband, not my girlfriend, not my wife. Not my wife!

How have I lived this long making breakfast in bed for every lover I've ever had, and none of them, until this morning, has ever done that for me?

Is it possible that Helena is different from my wife not only in ways that make me sad, but also in ways that could make me happy?

I decide to stay at Helena's until it's warm enough for a swim. Helena clicks on the TV, turns on *America's Top Model*. "My guilty pleasure," she says, eyes glued to the screen. Weird, I think, and I eat my breakfast, savoring every bite.

SUDDENLY I HAVE A GIRLFRIEND.

True to the lesbian stereotype—"What do lesbians bring to their second date? A U-Haul"—Helena starts sleeping over at the Bungalito several nights a week. It's good for both of us. I get to sleep with her, and she cuts half of her commute to the seven a.m. "click-in" at SoulCycle in Beverly Hills.

I clear a couple of drawers for Helena's Invisalign trays and her backup SoulCycle sweats and Prada sunglasses. I stock her fat-free yogurt and her fresh-ground peanut butter in my fridge. I learn to spread my homemade orange marmalade paper-thin on her 80-calorie Ezekiel toast. Weeknights we sleep in Silver Lake.

Weekends we hang out at her house, eating takeout, watching TV, floating in her pool.

Except for that first sleepless night in Helena's bed, for reasons I don't understand, I sleep more deeply than I ever have when Helena spoons me all night. On Sundays she picks me up after my Al-Anon meeting and we take the 101 to the 110 to the 10 to the 405 to the Westside to meet her sister for a two-hour ocean-view hike. Helena and her sister are very grown-up—sunscreened and REI-attired, successful, financially secure, their closets full of pumps and skirt suits, primed for affluent retirements. Sometimes, chugging up the mountain between them with my bare, sun-spotted face and my thrift-store yoga pants, I feel like a child on a nature outing with her parents.

My fridge dies, and Helena sends me a link for the perfect replacement. My laptop crashes, and she drives from Sherman Oaks to Silver Lake to lend me hers. Helena's a businesswoman, but she loves that I'm a writer, and she loves my writer's life and my writer friends, and she loves my writing. When I get home from a month at an artists' colony she begs to read the terrible first draft of my new novel, a draft not even my agent has seen. I leave her at the Bungalito, reading, and go out to get my nails done so I don't hang over her, watching her face. While I'm sitting in the salon's vibrating chair, my phone keeps lighting up with texts from Helena, screenshots of the paragraphs she loves most.

For our first Christmas I give Helena a silly wool hat for "chilly" SoulCycle mornings. She gives me La Perla lingerie. She makes me a set of keys to her house and I make her a set of keys to mine. She invites me to spend days writing beside her pool, and on those days she fills her fridge with my favorite treats.

When my frozen East Coast friends come to town for a book tour or a Southern California thaw-out, Helena buys good steaks and good booze and throws them pool parties and goes to their events and buys multiple copies of their books.

HELENA PRIDES HERSELF on not having had "work done." But one night she shows up at the Bungalito looking several years younger than she did two nights earlier. When I comment on that, she tells me that a nurse friend came over for dinner and injected some filler into her cheeks.

"You got shots? In your *face*?"

"Of course I did. Everyone you know gets filler and Botox. You think Darcy was born with those lips? Didn't you ever notice that Lolly's forehead never moves?"

Helena squints at my face. "You could get rid of those laugh lines, you know," she says.

"I'm never doing that. I earned my wrinkles. I'm not getting shots in my face to hide them."

"Okay, Berkeley." Helena calls me "Berkeley" whenever I express an opinion that's more radical than hers, which happens pretty much all the time. "Trust me," she says. "It's only a matter of time."

I've always been overly influenced by my lovers, one of many bad habits I'm trying to break this time around. Despite my best intentions, though, I can't seem to stop staring into the mirror, pulling back the loose skin on my face to see what I'd look like without those laugh lines. I start asking my friends if they've had filler or Botox. Except for Charlotte, every one of them confesses to that and more.

Gorgeous forty-year-old Darcy tells me she stops by her dermatologist's office for "booster shots" at least once a month "on my way home from Whole Foods." Forty-five-year-old Geneen, a women's empowerment coach, tells me she's been getting Botox since she was twenty-seven. Lolly flips through her phone and shows me photos of her neck before and after surgery. Even Hannah confesses to having had a face-lift at age forty-five, when she was working in Hollywood, "sitting in writers' rooms full of thirty-year-olds."

I Google "feminism and plastic surgery" and discover, to my mortification, that Gloria Steinem has had what she describes as "a little nip/tuck."

"A few years ago, during a brief stint hosting the *Today* show on NBC," *The Guardian* reported in November 2011, "she had a little fat removed from around her eyes so, as she once put it, 'I didn't look like Mao Tse-tung and I could wear my contacts.'" But she looked worse afterward, which confirmed Steinem's decision not to have more extensive surgery. "And what I care about is the message, and I realize that if I had plastic surgery, it would just distract people. It would be like having a bad toupee; they wouldn't listen."

In 2009, the National Organization for Women, which once campaigned against plastic surgery, reversed its position. "Middle-aged women are struggling to compete in the job market," NOW president Terry O'Neill told *The Nation*, "and cosmetic surgery can help them appeal to employers."

In my favorite "aging humorously" memoir, *I See You Made an Effort: Compliments, Indignities, and Survival Stories from the Edge of 50*, I find this.

"It wasn't until I hit forty that I started to look at my face critically," author Annabelle Gurwitch writes, and I think, Forty? Apparently I'm twenty years late. No wonder Helena's on my case. "I've had things injected in my face that I wouldn't clean my house with."

Of her decision to surrender to the knife, Gurwitch writes, "It only took forty minutes to take out the bags I had spent forty years accumulating . . . I wrestled with a case of buyer's remorse. Had I tampered with an essential part of myself?"

Gurwitch's reflections don't scare me off. I've spent the past couple of years deliberately tampering with—and becoming more intimate with—inner parts of myself, so the thought of tampering with the outside doesn't worry me as much as it might.

Once I know what's keeping not only my beautiful friends but also my feminist icons beautiful, I can't un-know it. If it works for them, politics notwithstanding, why would I deprive myself of putting it to work for me?

Of all my "fixed" friends, Lolly is closest to my age, and her "work" looks the most natural, so I make an appointment with her plastic surgeon, whose office is on Rodeo Drive.

Just like in the movies: as I'm waiting in Dr. Weiss's minimalist, security-guarded lobby, the elevator doors open, ejecting a tall, thin woman in a wide-brimmed black hat, huge black sunglasses, and a bandaged face. I can't help myself. I peek to see if she's *someone,* but she ducks her head and scurries out of the building. I watch through the tinted plate-glass windows as a uniformed chauffeur jumps out of a waiting butter-yellow Jaguar, opens the rear door, and gently helps her in. I can't believe that this woman and I have anything in common. I just wish it was the car and not the doctor.

"I'm here for a consult," I tell Dr. Weiss, a man who seems to be in his forties but whose face is so smooth, I wonder if he might be operating on himself.

He hands me a round mirror. "What's bothering you?" he asks.

"Growing old in a town that worships youthful beauty," I answer.

Dr. Weiss smiles and waits.

"Aren't *you* supposed to tell *me* what's wrong with my face?" I say.

"There's nothing wrong with your face. I'm just here to help you feel more comfortable with what you see in the mirror."

I sigh and point to the lines between the edges of my mouth and my nose. Dr. Weiss nods. Then I point to the wrinkles at the sides of my eyes. He nods again. "What would it cost to fix all that?" I ask.

"I'm giving you the friends-and-family discount, since Lolly referred you," he answers. "So it would be eight hundred and fifty dollars."

"What about my lips?"

Dr. Weiss squints at my mouth through his magnifying head lamp. "I could give you a bit of Restylane, but that's it. We don't want you looking like Daffy Duck."

I close my eyes for a moment and I see the way Helena ducks her head when I try to kiss her, when I ask her if she wants to have a sexcapade with me this weekend. Would a few shots of toxins in my face give me more of a shot with Helena? Could she be that superficial? Could I?

"Do it," I say.

"Are you sure? You said you were here for a consult."

"I'm sure."

A few days later, when the swelling goes down, I look at myself in the mirror and I don't just feel more comfortable with what I see. I'm ecstatic with what I see. And I'm also totally weirded out by what I see, which is a person who looks a lot like me.

I can't believe I actually paid someone to *change my face*.

Helena comes over for dinner. I don't tell her what I did, and she doesn't notice. Or maybe she notices and doesn't say. Her obliviousness rolls off me. My problem with Helena can be solved, as Scarlett O'Hara would say, another day. I might not have gotten my girlfriend's attention, but at least I got a better face.

SOME OF MY FRIENDS don't like Helena. Some of them like her, but they don't like the way she talks to me. I know what they mean. Helena can be caustic and arrogant and withholding with her own emotions, even as she's fiercely advocating for mine.

My shitty opinion of myself, and attendant go-to strategy of blaming myself for everything all the time, drives Helena nuts. She campaigns ceaselessly against it. When I have a misunderstanding with a friend or a coworker, when I get an assignment from a new editor and my insecurities supersede my confidence, when a single gray day makes me kvetchy and blue, Helena becomes my personal translator, interpreting my motivations and actions far more positively than I can. She's a fixer of problems logistical, technological, and professional, an installer of streaming TV players and timesaving iPhone apps, a steadfast friend, a tireless hiking buddy, an Olympic-level mom.

Therein lies the rub. I love sleeping—*sleeping*—with Helena, and baking cookies for Helena, and shopping for Bungalito furnishings with Helena, and being coddled and spoiled by Helena, and coddling and spoiling her. Sadly, none of this adds up to passion, to whispered midnight intimacies, to lust. It's not magic between Helena and me. Helena and I don't look into each other's eyes and say, "I love you." We say, "Love you" to each other, the way my brother and I do.

Helena doesn't like to kiss or walk with our arms around each other or hold hands. When we're at a party or hanging out with friends, we're usually on opposite sides of the room. One night she takes me to happy hour at the piano bar in the lobby of the Beverly Wilshire, and the Old Hollywood vibe gets me so excited, I jump into her lap. With stiff arms and tight lips, she removes me. "I don't do that in public," she says.

I find myself acting out in small, sometimes dangerous ways, trying to shock Helena into . . . what? Becoming someone she's not? Feeling things she doesn't? I go rogue while we're hiking, leaving Helena on the authorized trail, bushwhacking my way up the mountain through the sagebrush, determined to touch the Hollywood sign. A helicopter overhead chops the silence, blaring a warning that I'll be arrested if I don't leave the area *now*. I slip and slide all the way down the hill, dust myself off, find myself bloodied and bruised. "Scofflaw," Helena says, shaking her head.

I ride my bike to the Nokia Theatre and sneak into the Emmy Awards, posing as a geriatric paparazzo. Helena laughs and admires my photographs of the dress rehearsal.

I cut off most of my hair. Helena doesn't comment.

I invite my friends to skinny-dip in Helena's pool, assuming it will make her uncomfortable. It doesn't.

I get judgy when a friend of hers gets too drunk at one of my parties.

My bad behavior bothers me more than it bothers Helena, probably because I understand what it means. I wish I were in love with Helena, but I'm not. I try everything I can think of to change that. I wear the La Perla. I bake the cookies. I buy the gifts. Nothing changes. I tell Helena what I feel, that we're twisting ourselves into knots, trying to be what we're not.

Helena disagrees. Even in her fighting to go on with me, she proves why we need to stop. She doesn't shout or cry; she makes rational arguments. She says I'm still hung up on my wife, idealizing my dead marriage, comparing her unfavorably and unfairly, She's right, of course. I plead guilty to all charges. Still, I feel what I feel and I want what I want, and I remain convinced I'll never have it with Helena.

She says passion is a flash in the pan. "Companionship," she says. "That's the lasting thing." I tell her that I understand her priorities, but they're not mine. I want a lover who walks through the door on fire to kiss me, a lover I'm on fire to kiss. I give her house keys back to her. She gives mine back to me.

Two days later Helena sends me a bouquet big enough to hide the man who delivers it, dozens of peonies and roses, long-stemmed, blushing white. The card says, "I love you. I'll try." I put the bouquet in my car and drive it to Clara's house, where it won't be beckoning at me, weakening my resolve to do the right thing. Clara takes the flowers, shaking her head.

"What?" I say.

"Do you really want to know what I think?"

"Maybe," I say.

"Helena's great," Clara says. "The two of you are great together. And you're doing to her what your wife did to you."

"Huh?"

"Six months ago you were begging your wife to take your calls," Clara says. "Now Helena's begging you to take hers."

"One thing has nothing to do with the other," I say. Driving home, breathing in the lingering scent of all those flowers, I can't help but wonder if Clara's right.

I CREATE A NEW PROFILE on OKCupid. I start going to restaurants with strangers—female strangers this time, because I'm looking for more than hot sex, although I wouldn't turn it down. None of the women I meet is anywhere near as smart, lively, or loving as Helena. None of them knows what's going on with my job, which is getting weirder and weirder by the day. I'm not used to filling my weekends the way I did in my first months in L.A., going to movies alone, tagging along with coupled friends. Sundays are endless again.

Clara asks if I want the vase back, now that Helena's bouquet has died. "Don't you miss her?" she asks. "Jules and I do."

What sane sixty-two-year-old rejects love and commitment and armloads of peonies in hopes of finding something everyone wants and almost no one has? A few weeks after our breakup, I e-mail Helena and ask if she'd consider doing a couples counseling session with me. I send her a link to the Beverly Hills therapist who saved a friend's marriage.

"Just tell me when and where," she writes back immediately. "I'll be there."

Even as I'm figuring out what to wear to the session, I'm wondering: Mascara or not? Waterproof or not? Why am I doing this?

Driving west on Beverly, wondering.

Circling the therapist's block an hour early, wondering.

I'm still wondering when I hear a familiar honk. I glance into my rearview mirror and there's Helena, right behind me. She pulls her car up next to mine and she rolls down her window and she smiles her familiar smile, and she says, "Hi, honey," in her familiar way. She beckons for me to follow her into a garage and she pays for both of us and we get out of our cars and she holds her arms out to me and I fall into them with an equal mix of gratitude and despair. Who gets two great loves in one lifetime? I was lucky to have had one.

After the session, to celebrate our reconciliation, Helena takes me to the Polo Lounge at the Beverly Hills Hotel. Sipping Champagne cocktails on the patio with white linen napkins in our laps and bougainvillea draping the curvy white walls, trying not to stare at the celebrity couple whose names we can't quite remember, I imagine my wife—or is that God?—looking down at me, shaking her head or His head, reminding me that I used to spend my nights out with my wife at indie movie houses and Occupy encampments, drinking Two-Buck Chuck and feeling like the luckiest woman alive. And now? And now the Polo Lounge, feeling like the most ambivalent woman alive.

SEVENTEEN

The minute I arrive at the Bellissima office, I can tell something's wrong. It's too quiet. No one's at her desk. I check my phone to see if I forgot a company-wide meeting. No.

The lunchroom's empty. That never happens first thing in the morning. I go looking for my boss. Heather's office is empty. Her little antique side table, the artwork on the walls, the pictures of her kids are all gone.

"Heather left," Marguerite says from behind me.

I turn to face Marguerite. Her eyes are red and puffy. "We had a meeting about the spring line yesterday," I say. "She didn't tell me she was leaving."

Marguerite dabs at her cheeks with a pretty white hankie. Heather showed me that hankie in our meeting yesterday. She asked me to research the history of handkerchiefs for the spring line.

"Did you know she was quitting?" I ask Marguerite. "Did she get another job?"

Marguerite shakes her head. "Check your e-mail."

I go back to my desk. The memo from Isabel to the whole company says that Heather left "for a new opportunity." It says that everyone who reported to Heather—Marguerite, Clementine, and me—will report directly to Isabel from now on.

My anxiety skyrockets. Nearly thirty years ago I worked for a cool company much like Bellissima. We had a staff of groovy artists and writers who produced a groovy catalogue full of groovy travel clothes made of all-natural fabrics. Then a giant corporation bought our cute little company, and within six months, the groovy clothes and the groovy catalogue and the groovy people, including me, were all gone.

It was horrible when it happened, but I was in my thirties. I freelanced for as long as I could hold out, and then I got another job. I'm in my sixties now, unemployable. I moved to L.A. for this job. I bought a house for this job. This job pays for that house.

Isabel's a real person, I tell myself. A nice person. With good politics and good values. There's no way she'd sell the company to some evil corporation. The intuition that tells me otherwise must be paranoia.

BUT THEN A WEEK LATER Isabel summons me to her office and closes the door. She sinks to the floor with her legs folded in half lotus, as usual, and gestures for me to join her there, as usual. The look on her flawless face tells me what I don't want to know.

"Meredith." She sighs. "You've been doing a great job. You've given the company a voice. The perfect voice for us, really. You've taught us so much about using a few words to convey big ideas."

"That's good to hear," I say through clenched teeth.

"The thing is . . ." Isabel picks at a loose white thread on her shredded jeans. "Everyone's doing eco-clothing now. The market is saturated. If we're going to stay competitive, we need to make some big investments in R&D."

"Uh-huh."

"We need to cut back on payroll so we can afford to do that."

My lunch roils in my belly. My free, company-wide Indian lunch, eaten just an hour ago with my fellow Bellas.

"I'm so, so sorry," Isabel says. "But we're going to have to let you go."

Don't cry don't cry don't cry.

"If I'm not here," I manage, "who's going to do the writing?"

"Each department is going to write its own copy."

"The designers are going to write copy? The merchandisers? The *sales reps*?"

"They know the products," Isabel says.

"They don't know how to *write*."

"They'll learn."

Does Isabel actually believe the all-too-popular excuse for not paying writers, that the craft of writing is "providing content," and therefore something anyone can do?

"Effective when?" I choke out.

"Effective now," Isabel says. "Norma's waiting for you in the HR office."

She unfolds her long legs and unfurls her body in one smooth move, leaving a scattering of short white threads on the carpet where she was sitting. "The two of you can work out the details."

How am I going to feed myself? Pay my therapist? *Keep the Bungalito?*

Stiffly, I push myself to my feet, wincing at the shooting pains in my knees. I want to say something. Something angry, something graceful, something self-possessed. But I'll cry if I try to speak.

"I'm sorry," Isabel says again as I head for the door.

I don't answer. I send a text to Charlotte—"Got fired, outta here"—and decide to skip the HR office and get out of the building before I fall apart.

I CALL HELENA from my car. When I hear her voice, I start to cry.

"I lost my job."

"*What?* You just got a great review! What reason did they give you?"

"Budget cutbacks."

"Not your performance?"

"No."

"Okay, good. You can get unemployment. Where are you right now?"

Normally I hate it when Helena uses her steely business-woman voice with me. But now it soothes me. "Driving home."

"Who fired you?"

"Isabel."

"Did she give you anything in writing?"

"No."

"Did you sign anything?"

"No."

"Good. I'll meet you at the Bungalito."

Twenty minutes later I'm on my couch with Helena, crying and shaking. "I'm too old to get another job," I weep.

"You'll go back to freelancing. And your unemployment will almost cover your mortgage."

"That only lasts six months. What if I lose the Bungalito?"

"That's not going to happen."

Helena stands.

"I'm taking you to dinner. Wherever you want to go." She pulls me to my feet. Her cavalier attitude infuriates me. Why is she always minimizing my crises?

"I'm too upset to go out to eat," I say.

Helena laughs. "When were you ever too upset to eat?" She puts her arm through mine and steers us toward the door. "You'll feel better tomorrow," she says, opening the passenger door of her Mercedes for me.

I DON'T FEEL BETTER the next day. I feel terrified and bereft. How could this have happened, again? A plan in place, a life running smoothly, a sense of safety in the world, and then—gone. Again.

Helena calls. Her voice is soothing, but I don't hear her words. All I hear is the voice in my head saying, *I love her and she loves me, but she is not my person.*

Stop catastrophizing, I tell myself. Don't turn one bad thing into everything bad. You don't have to lose your girlfriend just because you lost your job.

"Honey?" Helena says.

"I'm here," I say, painfully aware that "here"—being in my six-ties; having a girlfriend I'm not in love with; being unemployed; being utterly uncertain about pretty much everything important in my life—is not where I want to be.

I can do something about one of those things. I tell Helena I'll call her later and I send out a mass e-mail, telling friends that I'm going to be freelancing again, asking them to send work my way. Over the next few days I get a dozen responses from writers and editors across the country, people I've read, reviewed, fed, housed, and written for and people who have read, reviewed, fed, and housed me.

Another item for the list of Good Things About Getting Old: in sixty years, one amasses sixty years' worth of colleagues, friends, and goodwill—many of whom, I learn from their return e-mails, are going through major life changes, too.

Carol, who's fifty-nine, tells me that she just left the lucrative corporate accounting job that bored her and went after a job she really wanted, managing expenses for an indie film.

"I could have hung in there a few more years and then retired," she says. "But I don't even know what retirement *means* for some-one like me. Why would I stop working when I'm at the top of my game? I've never been as skilled or as smart as I am now."

A week later, Carol e-mails her friends to tell us that she beat out fifteen younger candidates for her dream job on her dream show—which, as it turns out, shoots in New York. Carol has lived in L.A. for thirty years; none of her friends, including me, are happy to see her go. "I'll come home for Christmas," she prom-ises, and recruits a bunch of us to pack up her duplex so she can list it on Airbnb.

My fifty-five-year-old friend Lolly is leaving her husband of twenty years. After a decade of ambivalence and marriage counseling and romantic escapes that were neither romantic nor an escape, Lolly hung it up. "Jim's my best friend," she tells me. "We have grandkids together. I can't stand the idea of erasing all that history. But being married to my best friend isn't good enough. I want to be madly in love again before I die."

Eighty-two-year-old Mary, whose first book was an international bestseller and whose second and third books weren't, was my Berkeley writing buddy. When I moved to L.A., Mary moved under duress, too. "I did the math," she told me. "I had $80,000 in savings. With my pension and Social Security, I could make that last about three years in Berkeley.

"I figured I had two choices. I could keep renting a $3,200 Berkeley studio for two more years, then kill myself when I ran out of money. Or I could live someplace affordable until I'm ready to die." Mary moved to the small town in Oregon where her daughter and grandson live. She rents a two-bedroom house there for $550. "I'm keeping your Hendrick's and your martini glass in the freezer," she told me, "in case you feel like driving four hours to Butt-Fuck Oregon to drink with me."

My fifty-five-year-old bestie, Celia, spent two years and much of her savings starting a small restaurant, then chucked it for a nonprofit job. At sixty, Naomi quit her union job as a script supervisor and started working on call so she can write a memoir about her childhood in a kibbutz "while I can still remember what happened." Fifty-one-year-old novelist Dana, my first Bungalito guest, took out a second mortgage on her Brooklyn apartment and spent a year watching *The Sopranos* in one-minute intervals, teaching herself to write for TV. Then she wrote a pilot based on her novel, sold it to HBO, and started earning more money per episode than she'd made as a novelist in a year.

These reports calm and console me. Clearly I'm not the only old fart whose life is continuing to take young-fart turns. If I'm going to be reduced to a cultural stereotype, the "sixty is the new forty" demographic isn't a bad club to join. The changes my friends are making scare them, too. It gives me courage to see them acting on their determination, pushing past their fear.

HEARING MY NEWS, local friends rally round. They tell me I'll be happier being a "real writer," cook me dinners, buy me drinks, walk me up and down mountains until my anxiety dissolves into cardio overload. I'm blown away by the quality of the friendships I've built in two short years.

I'm surprised, too, to realize that, through no particular effort of my own, most of my new friends are in their thirties and forties. Maybe that's a function of my denial about my actual age, or my propensity for hiking steep mountains, celebrating happy hour religiously, and exchanging the grittiest sexual details.

And then there's this. I've grown close with a bunch of young women who see me as a spare mom. Jade, who's thirty-seven, calls me FM, for "Future Me." Charlotte's mother, whom I met when she visited from Boston, thanked me for "being such a good local mother" to her girl. Darcy and I talk about sex at a level of detail I've never shared with anyone, but she looks at me blankly when I mention the word *pain* in conjunction with sex. Molly introduced me at a book reading as her "writing mom." When I complained to Helena that I thought of these women as my friends, not my kids, she laughed and told me to be grateful they don't call me Grandma.

Helena has a point. Why should I care? If my young women friends love me in part because they're looking for mothering, I love them in part because I'm looking for young women to mother.

WITHIN A MONTH of sending out my SOS, I have a contract to edit a friend's sister's debut novel. Within two months I'm helping an actor's widow write her husband's biography. I'm not earning enough to replace my Bellissima income, but if I shop at Costco more and Yummy.com less, I'll be able to make it work for a while.

Once I would have rejected any financial plan that came with a life-span of "a while." I would have driven myself nuts looking for a more long-term, less anxiety-provoking solution. Now I know better. Long-term solution? Security? Stability? God laughs. So do I. These days my plan is this. If it's good enough for now, it's good enough for me.

I'VE BEEN WORRIED ABOUT MONEY all my adult life. Unlike my worries about my marriage, my most catastrophic money worries have never come true. The Holocaust mentality that was my inheritance kept fear on the payroll as my abusive coach, flogging me from the sidelines, keeping me focused on the next loss even as I was winning.

Now I know that when I stumble, when I fall, I get up and keep going. I know I'll do that again. The one thing I can't afford to lose now is time. I can't, I won't waste time worrying about money or anything else that doesn't pose an immediate, intractable threat.

I don't know how I'll make it without my job at Bellissima. It seems likely that job will be my last. Sixty might be the new forty, but a sixty-two-year-old without a job is commonly known as a retiree.

Still, whether it's fair or not (not), I'm a middle-class woman from a white upper-middle-class family, and—to state the often-ignored obvious—that gives me an advantage. I've never asked a loved one for a loan, and I hope I never need to. But I have friends and family who have enough—more than enough, some of them—and unlike less blessed sixtysomethings who tightrope-walk without that net, I have people and resources to break my fall.

Helena's right. I won't lose my house, and not because she'll pay the mortgage if I can't. Thanks to the dumb luck of my birth circumstances—my race; my parents' educations; an affluent, sophisticated childhood in one of the world's great cities; the feminist movement, which stuck its foot into some critical doorways just in time to let me in—even without a high school diploma or a financially advantageous marriage or the ability to keep a job for longer than two years, I've managed to support myself (and later, my children) since I left home at sixteen.

I own a 750-square-foot house in a neighborhood like so many other neighborhoods in "desirable" cities: "dangerous" until the white folks moved in, now increasing in value with the arrival of each beard-waxing barbershop, hot-yoga studio, and fresh-pressed juice bar. So yes, post-Bellissima, I've gone back to being a "starving artist." But chances are good that I'll never starve. And I've got a lot of help.

Al-Anon meetings help. They remind me that the object of the game is not an uninterrupted stream of good news and blissed-outedness, but the ever-improving ability to achieve and maintain serenity, whatever the news may be.

Forgive me, fellow twelve-steppers: alcohol helps. I've always enjoyed the warm, loose, truthy-blurty blur I find at the bottom of a martini glass. But since I arrived in L.A., where carbs are contraband, cocktails are compulsory, and everything stops for happy hour, every day of the week, alcohol has become the face I'm eager to see as I drive home at night, the hand I reach for as I walk in the door, a trusty companion who bats away the loneliness before it sinks its stinger into me.

Paradoxically, being old helps. In *Sidewalking: Coming to Terms with Los Angeles,* David Ulin, former book critic of the *Los Angeles Times*, quotes Orson Welles: "The terrible thing about L.A. is that you sit down, you're twenty-five, and when you get up you're sixty-two." The opposite is true of me. I got to L.A. and sat down at sixty, and now I'm getting up with the life of a twenty-five-year-old. Most of my fellow geriatric Americans are retiring from lifelong careers, not hustling to start new ones. I veered off the straight-line path, along with several hundred thousand members of my cohort, in the 1960s. Unlike most of them, I never veered back. So how surprising is it, really, that I don't find myself on a straight-line path to a well-funded retirement?

Also helpful: Helena's generous friendship and encouragement, even as I continue to doubt our compatibility as lovers.

God helps. Until my first night in Los Angeles, when I ran out of hope and ran into God in the middle of a dark night, I'd spent the past half century railing Bill Maher–style against "the opiate of the masses." Living in close-knit harmony with the God-fearing elderly African Americans in my Oakland neighborhood, I rued the fact that my neighbors were being suckered by the preacher man, giving God the glory instead of giving the One Percent hell.

Whoops. More and more often, these days, I'm able to practice Al-Anon's first line of defense, "turning it over"—to God, to fate, to a more benevolent universe than the one my persecuted progenitors inhabited. Doing that—even imagining doing that—actually helps.

Living in Los Angeles helps. What better place to start over than this city of reinvention, where people, and businesses, and the city itself slip into and out of identities with the ease and frequency of a costume change? So said Moby in *The New York Times*, in a story about droves of New York creatives moving to the Eastside of L.A. "Los Angeles is now where young artists can really experiment, and if their efforts fall short, it's not that bad because . . . almost everyone else they know is trying new things and failing, too."

What's not to love? L.A. is a bright grin of a city whose manmade miseries (paralyzing traffic, depressing strip malls, dangerous pollution, and did I mention soul-eating traffic?) and natural wonders (seventy miles of pristine, mostly public beaches on one side of town, and a 4,300-acre park with fifty mountain miles of hiking trails on the other) are blessed and bathed by the most show-offy weather God and climate change have to offer.

My Plan B life comes complete with blue sky, warm breezes, birdsong, and citrus-scented air. Plants that struggled for survival in the salty Bay Area chill grow here like kudzu. In the garden I planted, pink angel trumpets go limp and lovely in the afternoon sun. Leggy papyrus puffs wave in the warm breeze. Gardenia bushes sprout fragrant white blossoms; lemon, lime, and orange trees fruit throughout the year.

When I feel lonely, or when the Eastside heat hits the high nineties, I pack up and head for Hannah and Michael's house on the cooler, ocean-adjacent Westside. There I spend days writing on the antique olive-green velvet chaise that Hannah calls my "throne," spurred on by the keyboard clicks from her office down the hall. When the daylight goes dusky blue, Hannah and I cook simple-fancy dinners together from her *Silver Palate Cookbook*, peppered with the basil and thyme she grows in her backyard.

In my old life, I was my own bad boss. No later than six each morning, over my wife's sleepy protests, I slithered out of our warm bed, pulled on my threadbare cashmere socks, tiptoed upstairs, and stationed myself at my attic desk. There I stayed until I'd met the day's deadlines or until the sun set, whichever came first, refusing myself a meal at the kitchen table, let alone a midday hike with a friend.

Now I live in paradise. And now I'm too old for that shit. In three years, I'll be eligible for Medicare. In five years, if Social Security still exists, it'll cover half of my nut.

"I had come to the end of the line," I read in my current bedside companion, *Sidewalking*, "the place where the myths of possibility and reinvention butt up against the edges of the continent, and the vanishing point of the horizon becomes the vanishing point of the known world."

The vanishing point of my known world keeps moving, which is scary and disorienting, and keeps me on my slightly arthritic toes.

NOW THAT I'M FREELANCING AGAIN, I say yes to anyone who asks me to do anything interesting—even in the middle of a workday, and especially when the invitation is to something new: a "talk-back" screening of some hot series' next season on the Paramount lot, a talk by Anne Lamott or Mary Karr at the downtown public library, a lawn picnic and movie at the Hollywood Forever ceme-tery where Douglas Fairbanks, Jayne Mansfield, Rudolph Valen-tino, and Cecil B. DeMille were laid to rest.

When I was a teenager, my what-the-hell adventurousness was fueled by an age-appropriate assumption that I'd never grow old or die. Now my what-the-hell-ness is fueled by the opposite moti-vation, the fact of my impending mortality. Striking out as a sixteen-year-old in 1967, I cared only about what I got to feel and do—how many thrills I could cram into each day; how much war-and-inequality-busting I could get done while I was at it. Now that I'm a sixty-two-year-old, the family-building, career-building, marriage-building years are behind me. I'm not build-ing anything anymore, except bone density if I'm lucky. I'm back to where I started, a pleasure-seeking missile again.

At this stage of life, what else is there? Before I die, dammit, I'm going to have myself some mind-blowing adventures. If not now, when?

———

IF I HAVE TO GET OLD, at least my timing is good. Now's the best time ever to be old and female and bold. At eighty, Joan Didion's wearing big black shades in the pages of *Vogue,* modeling Céline haute couture. Harriet Doerr wrote *Stones for Ibarra,* her first book, at seventy-three. Judi Dench won her first Oscar at sixty-four; Glenn Close is going strong at sixty-nine. Distance swimmer (and TED speaker, and *Dancing with the Stars* competitor, and out lesbian) Diana Nyad made it from Cuba to Florida on her fifth attempt at age sixty-four. Iris Apfel is modeling jewelry at ninety-five.

The day I harvested my first crop of gray hairs was the day I went cynical on the cheery feminist declarations about women and aging. "Women may be the one group that grows more radical with age," Gloria Steinem said. Eve Ensler wrote, "It has taken me so many years to be okay with being different, and with being this alive, this intense." Christiane Northrup, queen of women's wisdom, promised, "Ageless living means . . . you have enough experience to know what's not worth worrying about and what ought to be your priorities."

Biggest. Surprise. Ever: That cheery feminist crap is true. For the first time since childhood, I'm responsible to no one. I can be Helena's girlfriend or break up with her without upsetting my kids or my own living situation or my finances. I can make money or rest on whatever laurels I've got without depriving anyone of anything. I can binge-watch *Girls* till midnight or go to sleep at nine. The bad news and the good news is the same. I have nothing and no one to lose.

———

EIGHTEEN MONTHS INTO OUR RELATIONSHIP, Helena and I are perched on leather-topped stools, bellied up to the gleaming mahogany bar at Cliff's Edge in Silver Lake. Friendly hipsters are munching on sautéed Brussels sprouts and Parker House rolls; friendly hipster bartenders are muddling exotic herbs into splashes of small-batch vodka and bourbon and gin. I'm on my second Upper West Side; Helena is nursing her first and last Lemon Drop of the evening. If, as Dr. Phil says, the past is the best indicator of the future, she won't finish it; I will.

"I want to talk about your drinking," Helena says.

I stare at her, dumbstruck. "Where's this coming from?" I ask.

"You turn distant when you drink," Helena says. "You're like a different person. A person I don't much like."

My heart sinks. A cocktail-free future flashes before my eyes. It's not a welcome sight.

AS A CHILD OF THE SIXTIES, I came of age seeing alcohol as "the man's" drug, a soporific meant to mollify the masses, like religion and *Ozzie and Harriet* reruns. Our parents drank to get blotto, to feel and know *less* about themselves and the world. We did pot and hash and hallucinogens to feel our feelings *more*, to expand our consciousness, to see through lies and delusions: the government's, our parents', our own.

When I aged out of the youth movement, I started warming up to drinking. Getting buzzed no longer felt like an act of activist or artistic submission; it felt like a nice way to wind down at the end of a long day. Wine with dinner proved the gateway drug to a cocktail before dinner, sometimes after. More than once, during the war years with my wife, I brought a bottle of wine to her place in the guest-room bed.

But when I moved to L.A., alcohol and I got serious, fast. All those happy hours with strangers I hoped to convert to friends. All those unhappy hours in my rented apartment, alone. All those nights with nothing to look forward to.

I'm not about to admit this to Helena, but I've been a little worried about how much I love to drink. I'd devised a little test that I self-administered whenever my concern about my drinking exceeded the carefree pleasure I took from its effects. I'd tick off the differences between me and the alcoholics I knew, giving myself a get-out-of-sobriety-free card for each one.

I'd never had a blackout or an overdose or even a hangover. Check.

My drinking had never caused me to do anything I wish I hadn't: blow a secret, fall down, or puke. Check.

I'd never lost anything to my drinking—time, a job, a relationship, my car keys. Check.

I'd never gotten a DUI. Check.

Most significant—and this was my bright line, the notion to which I clung when I found myself counting down to happy hour at odd times of the day—*no one had ever expressed concern about my drinking.* How could I have a drinking problem when my drinking had never bothered me or anyone else?

Until now.

"You check out when you're drinking," Helena adds. "You're unreachable. It makes me feel alone."

Everything in me rises up against the sickening realization that I've just flunked my own test. My bright line has been crossed. Only one thing can save my relationship with the sexy, sweaty martini glass in front of me. Helena has to take it back.

"Of *course* I'm different when I drink," I say. "That's the whole point of drinking. Why would I guzzle all those liquid calories if I wanted to stay the same?"

"What's so bad about being who you are?" Helena says.

Despite my frequent complaint that Helena doesn't go deep enough, when she does, I see now, I don't like that, either.

I stroke her arm, lower my voice. "How can you feel alone? I'm right here."

Helena shakes my hand off. "I don't care what you do when you're alone or with your friends. But from now on, you can either drink or you can spend time with me."

I look longingly at my cocktail. A drop of condensation traces a trail down its contours, gathers, plops onto the dark wooden bar. And then I do something I've gotten good at doing since life took a turn on me: I adapt to current circumstances. I draw a new bright line.

"Okay," I say.

"Okay what?" Helena asks. I'm not surprised by her skepticism. Quick compliance is not exactly my groove.

"Okay, I won't drink when we're together."

"Really?"

"Really." I beckon to the bartender. "Can you bring me a boring-ass Perrier?" I say, pushing my cocktail toward him. He nods sympathetically and takes my happiness away.

———

A FEW NIGHTS LATER Helena and I are at a bar with friends, waiting for our table. Helena does not look happy. I follow her frown to the half-drunk martini in front of me. Of course I ordered it, and of course I drank half of it. But I didn't do either of those things consciously. Without even realizing what I was doing, I broke a promise to Helena and to myself. That scares me.

It scares me enough to make me decide to stop drinking—not only when I'm with Helena, but all the time.

THE FIRST NIGHT without a drink is pure hell. I feel like I'm depriving myself of pleasure for no good reason. I channel my frustration into moving my booze from the kitchen to the storage room under the house. It helps a bit not to find myself eye to eye with a bottle of Bulleit every time I open the pantry door. But I'm still tense, edgy, angry. The second night is worse.

Jesus, I think on the third night, speed-spooning Ben & Jerry's into my mouth in front of the open freezer, I really am addicted to drinking.

On the fourth night I have a prearranged date with Charlotte. She suggests happy hour, of course. I counterpropose a movie.

"I'm not drinking right now," I say.

"That's so great!" she exclaims.

"What's so great about it?"

"I wish I could stop drinking."

"Why?"

"It would be good for me. I wouldn't be so . . . fuzzy at night. And maybe I'd lose some weight. And . . . I don't know. It just seems *wrong* that I have a drink almost every night."

"Why don't you stop, then?" I ask.

After a long silence, Charlotte says, "I don't know."

EVERY MORNING I PROMISE MYSELF a Hendrick's martini that night. And then I realize that I don't want one martini; I want two or three or four. I want no limits. I want to dose myself with exactly as much oblivion as I choose. Knowing this makes it easier to live one more day and one more day without happy hour, without Hendrick's, without that blessed nightly "I'll think about it tomorrow" haze.

Not drinking stops sucking so badly after a couple of weeks. I actually start to enjoy the discipline of it, and the simplicity. It leaves me fewer choices to make. Instead of choosing between driving to meet a friend for happy hour and spending twenty bucks on an Uber, I'm driving. Simple. When I get there, I don't have to choose from an irresistible list of cocktails; I'm having a cranberry and soda with lime. Simple.

Not so simple: I stopped drinking, ostensibly, to save my relationship with Helena. But absent the buzzed blur, I find it harder to ignore what's missing between us. "Good enough" was good enough when I was drinking. Sober, I'm painfully aware of what I don't feel.

EIGHTEEN

have news," Hannah greets me, standing in her doorway, watching me schlep my stuff up her driveway. I'm here for an impromptu Memorial Day writing weekend, inspired by the current heat wave—otherwise known as late spring in Los Angeles. It was 99 degrees when I left Silver Lake.

"Let me guess," I say sarcastically. "You got AC."

Hannah has lived in L.A. all her life, and she's never lived in a house with air conditioning or heat. Until ten years ago, she says, she never missed them. Post–climate change, she has electric heaters going all winter and fans going all summer.

"Sorry. No." Hannah follows me into the house and gestures at her newly recovered white couch. "Have a seat."

A frisson of fear runs through me. That's what my dad used to say when he was about to administer my latest punishment. Hannah sinks into the matching "chair and a half" across the coffee table from me, her shoulders squared, her eyes locked on mine.

"You're not going to like this," Hannah says. "But I promise it's gonna be okay."

Hannah and I are so different, I don't know how we manage to be so close. If I were about to tell her something she didn't want to hear, I'd be having a twitchy, codependent fit, all insecurity and guilt. Not Hannah. Once she's decided she's doing the right thing, she marches into battle fully fortified, sans doubt or remorse. I attribute at least some of our dissonance to the difference between New York Jews—real Jews like me, that is—and L.A. Jews like Hannah. The West Coast version seems to me a diluted, imitative, sweeter version of the original, like those hipster brands of cream soda or Noah's "New York" Bagels. In New York, the city adapts to the Jews, which is probably why Lenny Bruce said, "If you live in New York, even if you're Catholic, you're Jewish." In L.A., the Jews adapt to the city.

"Earth to Meredith?" Hannah says.

"I'm listening."

"Michael and I are moving," Hannah says.

My mouth goes dry. "To Silver Lake?" *Fuck. Fuck. Fuck.* "It's about time you came over to the light side."

Hannah hates L.A. She grew up here, got temporarily rich writing a sitcom, divorced her stand-up comedian husband, and married salt-of-the-earth Michael, an ER doc. She hates everything I love about the city: the heat, the sun, the density, the sheen of brash style. Hannah made me feel at home in Los Angeles when I arrived from Northern California, and she's always dreamed of retiring to the place I left. I've coped with her threatened desertion by telling myself she'd change her mind, or she wouldn't leave till after I die, or there would be a nuclear war before she could carry out her nefarious plan.

"Michael got a job in Santa Cruz. We're buying a house there."

As this information moves from my ears to my brain to my solar plexus, Hannah keeps talking. "It's only a five-hour drive from here. Six at the most."

"When are you—?" *Leaving,* I cannot say.

"In two weeks. The hospital wants Michael there ASAP."

"Two weeks?"

"Don't freak out. I'll come to L.A. at least once a month," Hannah says. "I'll stay at your place. We'll have our pajama parties there instead of here. You'll hardly even know I'm gone."

"I'm happy for you," I say, meaning it. "I'm proud of you guys," I add. At sixty, she and Michael derive much of their happiness from the rebar of routines that keep their lives in place. Now they're throwing themselves, their two dogs, and their cat into the situation they normally do everything to avoid, dramatic change.

"Happy" is also the worst possible description of how I feel—for me.

Since I moved to L.A. two years ago, Hannah's house, Hannah's kitchen, Hannah's guest room—and most of all, Hannah herself—have been my anchors, my solid ground. But right now it's grown-up time at the O.K. Corral. My dear friend and her beloved husband are getting what they've always wanted. Mustering a *mazel tov* is the least I can do.

"You still talk to your Bay Area friends on the phone all the time," Hannah points out. "We'll stay connected the same way."

We both know this won't work. Hannah's my age. She and I don't do digital. We have an in-the-flesh, analog friendship. We're a pair of bears, keeping each other and our cave warm. We eat her quiche or my cookies while bitching about publishing. We host writers' brunches together. We meet up at our mutual friends' book readings at Book Soup, halfway between her side of town and mine. We go shopping at the fancy furniture store she loves, and she teaches me about fabric as we browse. She arrives early for Bungalito parties so I can put tinted moisturizer on her face and mascara on her lashes. And we do what we're supposed to be doing right now: spend a day or a weekend together, writing and cooking and talking and laughing.

Michael wanders into the living room and waves in my general direction, averting his eyes. Michael is a savant at emergency medicine and a profoundly shy, socially awkward man. The three of us have been in the same house at the same time on many occasions, and not once before has he entered a room in which Hannah and I were having a conversation. I'm guessing he's here to provide backup for his wife, which is so sweet in so many ways, it makes me even more determined to get over myself and give them my heartfelt blessing.

"Michael," I say, imitating the witty, composed adult I wish I were, "you cannot possibly be serious about taking Hannah away from me."

Michael regards me somberly. And then he nods. "Yes," he says. "Yes, Meredith, I am."

Hannah laughs nervously. Michael watches her watching me, his eyes moist with worry. I laugh, too, which beats the hell out of crying.

"Tell me everything," I say around the lump in my throat and the panic fluttering in my chest.

It's hard to concentrate as Hannah pulls out her phone and shows me the huge, *Grey Gardens* house on eight acres that she and Michael are buying, the renovations she's planning, the fourth bedroom she's calling mine. I'm trying to imagine my life in L.A. without Hannah's kitchen, Hannah's guest room. Without Hannah. We're all at our best with people who like and admire us. I'm at my best with Hannah. So is Helena. Seeing Helena shining under Hannah's light always makes me—made me—like Helena more. Now I won't be seeing Helena or myself in Hannah's beaming gaze anymore.

Just as Patricia's encouragement kept me in my marriage, Hannah has been the biggest booster of my relationship with Helena. Hannah tells me that I'm too picky, that passion never lasts anyway, that Helena is a wonderful person who adores me, and I must be suffering from postmarital PTSD to do anything other than stay with her.

I know that Hannah can and probably will keep singing Helena's praises from three hundred miles away. I also know that Hannah's departure will change things between Helena and me, just as my wife's prediction came true: although the shouting wasn't over for months, our marriage ended the day Patricia died.

"Look at that view," I say, pretending to study the pictures on Hannah's screen, while wondering if I will ever lose anything again without body-slamming into the memory of losing everything.

A FEW DAYS LATER Helena and I are taking her niece to the beach, so I'm in the backseat when I get a text from my friend William telling me that his husband, Armando, had a stroke a few hours ago. Armando is in the ICU at San Francisco General. "It's bad," William writes.

"No!" I cry out.

"What's wrong, honey?" Helena asks.

"Armando," I begin, and then my lips freeze, because Helena doesn't know who Armando is or what he means to me. She doesn't know that Armando and William were our witnesses when my wife and I got married in the Alameda County Clerk-Recorder's Office. She doesn't see the pictures in my head right now: Armando's brown eyes brimming with tears as the judge pronounced us "wife and wife." Armando's arms pulling my wife and William and my mother and me into a group hug. Armando wrapping himself in my wife's white wedding feather boa, white teeth flashing against his brown face.

"A friend . . ." I mumble, hunched over my phone, texting William, asking if there's anything I can do besides pray.

"Tell people," William texts back. By "people," he means our small circle of Bay Area friends, which includes my wife. My ex-wife, that is.

She and I haven't communicated in more than a year. The last time I e-mailed her, she asked me never to contact her again. But I want to call her right now, even though I'm in my new girl-friend's car, with my new girlfriend's niece, in the middle of my new life.

Bright, bouncy Armando hooked up to tubes and machines in an ICU? I cannot bear this thought. I certainly can't bear it alone. Ex-wife or not, she's the one I need to talk to.

"Are you okay?" Helena asks, her eyes on me in the rearview mirror. Her niece, whom I first met a few hours ago, swivels around to stare at me.

Who are these strangers, these people I've known for five

seconds, who don't know Armando or my wife or anyone I *really* love? Where are the people who know my history, the people who *are* my history? Not in this car.

"I'm fine," I say.

And then I text my wife—my ex-wife—because William asked me to.

"I have news about a friend of ours," I write. "Please get back to me as soon as you can."

Instantly, my phone pings. "Leaving right now!" my ex-wife replies. "Bringing food too."

My heart soars. So she knows about Armando, and she's already headed for the hospital. How could I have doubted her? She *is* the woman I knew her to be: rushing to be there for our dear friends, the men we chose to witness our marriage. Bringing food.

"So, so happy to hear that," I write back. "I knew you'd be a great help. Please give both boys a beso for me."

Waiting for her reply, I glance out the window. What I see—a caricature of a cute beach town—is utterly unfamiliar.

"Where are we?" I ask.

"Hermosa Beach," Helena says.

Still waiting for the gray dots to appear on my phone's screen, I map the distance between Hermosa Beach and LAX. Six miles. Helena could drop me at the airport. I could be in San Francisco in two hours.

"I'm on my way," I text my ex-wife. "See you ASAP."

I stare at my phone, waiting, my heart hammering in my chest. I wait. I wait. I ignore the chitchat between Helena and her niece, the sun blasting through the car window, the sweat running down my face. I have only one purpose: to wait for my wife's answer.

The gray dots appear. "Oops," my ex-wife writes. "That message wasn't meant for you. Not about the boys either."

I stare at my phone in disbelief. What just happened? For the first time in a year, with our dear friend in the ICU, my wife texted me by mistake?

Helena pulls into a parking lot carpeted with soft drifts of sand. Out the window a wide white beach is dotted with brightly colored umbrellas and blankets and towels and people throwing Frisbees. Between shoreline and horizon, surfers are poised on their boards, hands cupped and ready, heads craned around, looking to catch the next wave before it catches them.

"Overwhelmed," William texts me. "Will keep you posted."

Helena and her niece are rooting around in the trunk of the car. "Want your sweatshirt?" Helena calls to me. "It might get cold later."

Translation: it might get down to 70 degrees. What does Helena, native Angeleno, know about cold? About suffering?

"Yes, please," I say, and get out of the car.

AFTER WE'VE SHOWERED and taken Helena's niece to a rubbery lobster dinner at an imitation Maine lobster shack and dropped her at Helena's mom's house, Helena asks the usual question: whether I want us to spend the night at her place or mine.

"Neither," I say. "I'm going to stay at my house. By myself. I can't do this anymore."

"Do what?" Helena says.

"Be your girlfriend."

"That again." Helena starts the car.

"You've been so good to me," I say as we head east on the 110. "You believed in me so much, I started to believe in myself. But the way I love you—it's not the way I love. I might never love anyone that way again, but . . ."

"You're still in love with what's her name. Your imaginary, perfect *wife.*"

Helena's eyes gleam at me angrily. This, I know, is about as ugly as it's going to get. If she were a person who cried or yelled or begged, or I was a person who didn't, maybe I'd be in love with her. But she isn't. And I'm not.

"It's not fair," I say. "Your love gave me the confidence to leave you. I'm sorry."

"I'm sorry for *you*. You're fantasizing about a ghost."

I flash on the time early in our romance when I told my wife, "Being with you makes me act like a happier person than I actually am." I was laughing when I said it, but it was true. Her relentless good cheer convinced me that if I just faked it till I made it, eventually my nature would change. I wanted that. I wanted to live in the meadow, not the cave. I wanted to be like my wife: upbeat, fearless, calm. Who wouldn't choose that over being me?

I wouldn't. Not anymore. It's not the ghost of my wife I've been fantasizing about—it's the me I thought I could only be with her. I *am* that person now, without her. I'm that person now without Helena. I'm that person now.

"I want us to be friends," I say. "I know that sounds like bull-shit. But I mean it."

Helena doesn't answer. We crawl in tense silence through the perpetual logjam on the 110, creep north on the 101. We pass the Rampart exit, which always makes me think about "the Rampart police scandal," whatever that was, whenever that was. We pass the fountains shooting phallic plumes out of Echo Park Lake. We exit at Silver Lake Boulevard. We pass the Chilean-Italian-Mediterranean restaurant where Helena and I had a shitty makeup dinner after one of our shitty breakups.

Helena pulls up to the Bungalito, engine idling.

"Do you want to talk?" I say, because I love Helena, and because I've had my heart broken, so I can't stand breaking hers.

"Is there anything you haven't said?"

"You must feel it, too." I hear the pleading in my own voice: *absolve me.* "It's not right between us. But we could be friends."

"Be a big girl, Meredith," Helena says. "This is your decision, not mine. Own it."

I imagine my life without Helena in it. It doesn't look good. I know I have to do this, start all over again, again. I know I'm going to miss her and I know it's going to be a long, slow slog from where I am to feeling good. Again.

Decades ago, when my brother and I were both leaving our first marriages, breaking up our children's families, both of us racked by ambivalence and guilt, he said to me, "We're both so desperate for love, we can't leave when there's even a scrap of it left on the table."

That was thirty years ago. I want more than scraps now.

Helena pushes a button on her gleaming walnut dashboard. I hear the trunk pop open. "I'm pretty sure you're making a big mistake," she says.

Six months ago—six weeks ago, maybe—Helena's words would have chilled me to the bone. I would have rushed to call Hannah,

Celia, a few other trusted advisors. If they thought I should stay with Helena, I would have stayed with Helena.

"You might be right," I say.

I don't need to call anyone now. I get out of Helena's car and I take my backpack out of her trunk and I walk into my own house by my own self.

I want a drink, of course, by which I mean I want to start drinking and keep drinking until I fall asleep. But I don't have a drink and I don't eat a pint of ice cream. I take a hot bath and I close my eyes and sink into the soothing water and I pray to God that I've done the right thing, ending it with Helena, and I pray to God that someday I'll love someone wholly and passionately again.

NINETEEN

For the past two decades I've spent a few weeks each year at one of my favorite artists' colonies—little bits of heaven where the earthly needs of musicians, visual artists, and writers are handled by the talented, dedicated staff, leaving the artists with only two things to do: make art (or nap while dreaming of making art) and show up for dinner.

On a dare from Helena, I'd applied to a prestigious Vermont colony for the summer session. A few days after our breakup, I find a thick acceptance packet in my mailbox.

This is great news for my book deadline. For my anxiety management, not so much. Sitting down to dinner on the first night of a colony residency with Guggenheim fellows and Pulitzer Prize winners and MacArthur geniuses reminds me of walking into my junior high prom without a date, all eyes on my Brillo-pad hair, pimply face, and oh-so-wrong dress. After dinner most nights the residents gather in one another's studios for concerts, readings, dance performances, art exhibits, and film screenings of works destined for Carnegie Hall, the Tate, Cannes, the best-seller lists. Intimidating? Just a bit.

Making friends at a residency can go really, really well, as evidenced by my enduring colony friendships with Emily, Dana, and others. Or it can go really, really badly, as evidenced by the lonely residencies I've struggled through, writing in solitude all day, feeling like literature's greatest loser by night, soothed only by my frequent calls to my wife, who read me my mail, paid my bills, blew me kisses, and sent me back to my studio to do what I was there to do. When my social situation was particularly dire, she'd send extravagant care packages whose arrivals sparked curiosity and whose contents—Belgian dark chocolates, plump Turkish apricots, Japanese snack mix, French cheeses—provided instant cures for my unpopularity.

This time around I'll be walking that tightrope without a net. I instruct the post office to hold my mail, wish myself a fun, productive summer, and lug my seventy-five-pound suitcase to the airport in an eighty-dollar Uber, instead of sitting in the passenger seat of my wife's car.

Ten hours after takeoff from LAX, I take a deep breath and step into the colony dining room. Thirty strangers stop eating and talking and turn their eyes to me.

"I'm Meredith." I twist my face into a welcoming grin. "What's for dinner?"

Incredibly, everyone in the room smiles back at me. A raven-haired young woman with brilliant blue eyes jumps up and gives me a hug. "Welcome," she says. "I'm Marta. Novels and short stories. From Arizona."

"Tandy," says a woman who seems to be almost as old as I am. "Composer. Connecticut."

"C.J. Performance artist. Cairo."

"Justin. Painter. Williamsburg."

"Dawn. Playwright. Ann Arbor."

"Elaine. Filmmaker. Fort Greene."

"Miguel. Poet. I'm from Buenos Aires."

"Can I fix you a plate?" Marta asks me. "Would you like a glass of wine?"

It's been four months since alcohol has crossed the barrier between my longing and my lips. I have much to show for that time and that experience: a new awareness of what I use alcohol for (when drinking alone, to dull the loneliness; when drinking with others, to accelerate the fun) and the benefits of life without it (less insomnia, more productivity, and improved memory, a benefit whose value cannot be overstated for a woman my age whose father had Alzheimer's).

One of the slogans Helena brought home from SoulCycle was "How you do one thing is how you do everything." Despite the pleasure I take from skewering SoulCycle's pop-psych jargon, I've found this particular ditty to be true. The same way I struggle for balance between thinking long-term versus diving into the pleasures of the moment—settling for casual sex versus holding out for true love; breaking for fun on weekdays even when deadlines loom; planting perennials in my garden versus showy, instant-karma annuals—I struggle for balance between the pleasures of drinking and the benefits of not.

Yes, I'd prefer a lifelong relationship to a few hot nights in bed.

Yes, I'd rather live on in the literary canon than hear live reggae at the Bowl. Yes, I'd rather maintain my rep as a meeter of deadlines than inhale a noseful of orange blossoms. But I've learned this about medium-term living: being sixty means never having to say you're sorry for wanting it all, and going for as much of it as you can.

If I'd been planning on lifetime sobriety, I would have passed on the late-night boozy bonding sessions that make colony life what it is. But now that I know I can live without alcohol for months at a time, I feel ready to rejoin the party.

"Wine would be great," I say. "Thanks."

My first post-abstinence sip is at once anticlimactic and satisfying. It's just wine. It's just a slight boost to my mood, my confidence, my smile. Maybe I'll make it through the evening after all. Maybe I'll even make it through the summer without making the homesick kid's call home to wife/mommy. I hope so, since I'm all out of wives/mommies at the moment.

"ARE YOU SETTLING IN OKAY?" colony staffers ask each artist for the first few days after we arrive. "Is there anything you need?"

It's all I can do not to answer, "Are you fucking kidding me?" My studio has a bathtub in the bedroom, a leather chair facing a stone fireplace, and a loft with a sweeping view of the deer, foxes, and wild turkeys frolicking in the wildflower meadow that surrounds my own private aerie.

My book-in-progress is behaving itself, new pages stacking up day after day. I'm a member in good standing—good swimming— of the swim team, five very different women from three different countries who meet at four each afternoon to swim across an idyllic local pond. Driving there, packed into our subcompact rental car like half-naked clowns, Phoebe, Marta, Riya, Elaine, and I talk and laugh about our thickening bodies, our sex lives past, present, and imagined. Paddling through velvet water past loons and kayakers and jagged rock outcroppings, we continue the conversation. As the sun sinks, we swim back to shore, disembarking at the colony dripping wet, with dark wet breast spots blotching our sarongs, just in time for yet another sumptuous meal.

This is progress. This is a triumph. This is the best colony experience of my life. Without a wife or girlfriend playing backup, connecting me to the life I'll return to, I'm living the life I'm in, right here, right now. When my brain starts its minesweep for explosive thoughts, I take a breath, look around, and notice what a waste it would be to put my attention anywhere else.

Knowing that I'm here because the admissions committee valued my writing makes my writing better. Uninterrupted from dawn to dinnertime, I sink deep into the book I'm writing, finding its steady pulse each morning, right where I left it the night before. People here like me—they really, really like me! So there's no need to perform frantic circus tricks in hopes of winning their affection.

DURING MY SECOND WEEK in writers' paradise, I'm eating lunch at my desk when I get a text from Hannah.

"Michael just died," it says. "My world is over."

I stare at the words. They swim in front of me. I read them again.

Michael? Dead? That simply cannot be.

I dial Hannah's number. When she answers, I don't hear Hannah's strong, upbeat voice. I hear the ghost of Hannah, a stranger's whisper.

"Michael rode his bike to work this morning," she says in a low, halting monotone. "When he got there, he had a heart attack and fell onto the hospital steps. They worked on him and worked on him, but they couldn't—"

Hannah gasps, sobs, gulps.

"The doctors are—were—his coworkers. So they didn't want to stop trying. But there was nothing they could do."

"Honey." I can hardly speak myself. "How are you?"

I hear Hannah's panting breath: *Gasp-gasp-gasp*. Pause. *Gasp-gasp-gasp*. "Numb," she says. "Michael's boss is here, taking care of me. He gave me some pills."

"I'm glad you're not alone."

"My kids are coming."

"That's good."

I hear it again. *Gasp-gasp-gasp*. Pause. "We just started renovating the house. I'm sitting here in a construction site. By myself." A single sob bursts from her mouth. "I don't know what I'm going to do."

Three years ago, when I said, "I don't know what I'm going to do," to Hannah, she said, "You're going to get through this, I promise you."

"You're going to get through this, I promise you," I say to her now.

"I don't see how," she says.

I remember how comforting Hannah's solid presence was to

me, her big-boned body and goofy outfits and unglamorous dog, when we went for our hikes and threw our brunches and she showed me that my life in L.A. could be survivable, even good.

"I'll be there as soon as I can," I say.

"Stay where you are," Hannah says in that same flat, muffled voice. "There's nothing you can do. You have the whole summer ahead of you. Write your book."

"I can't be on the other end of the country while you're going through this."

"The pills . . . I'm falling asleep," Hannah mumbles, and hangs up.

I sit staring out my studio window. A family of wild turkeys pecks and struts its way across the meadow: an adult, a second, slightly smaller adult, and six identical chicks, in single file. I wonder if the big turkeys are mom and dad, mom and mom, or mom and a supportive friend. I wonder how the chicks know to walk that way, in perfect single file.

Didn't I have a conversation like this with my friend William a few weeks ago, while Armando was still in the ICU?

And another one, a couple of months ago, with the brother of my lifelong best friend? Cori and I walked to and from junior high together every day of seventh, eighth, and ninth grades. Over the next fifty years, whenever I came "home" to New York, my first stop was Grand Central, where Cori and I met to dream up our next adventure. Cori took the cover photos for three of my books, and loved me and fought with me and was there for me, and then she had routine surgery and stopped breathing on the operating table and died.

There was the call from the new boyfriend of my fifty-year-old colony friend Maggie, telling me that Maggie went out to walk their dogs through the woods near their Woodstock home and had a heart attack and died.

Not long ago, there was—and then there wasn't—my dad.

This was promised, and now it's happening. I'm older, and my people are older, and we've started dying off. Yes, we all feel like we have a whole lot more living to do, but tell that to the rotting temples of our bodies. There's a reason our grandmothers never uttered the word *menopause*. A hundred years ago, life expectancy for American women was forty to forty-five years. To our bodies, sixty is sixty. And for some of us, clearly, sixty is all we get.

Michael and Hannah just moved to their dream house, their dream life. Michael is—*was*—fifty-seven, a *doctor*, the healthiest living person I knew. He frowned when I sprinkled salt onto Hannah's thoughtfully unsalted chicken. He shook his head when I poured myself a martini from my BYO gin. He actually left the room when I took a spoon to my BYO Ben & Jerry's.

Michael's food intake never varied. His was a heart-healthy women's magazine diet, faithfully followed. Original Cheerios, sliced banana, 1 percent lactose-free milk for breakfast. Low-sodium sliced turkey on whole wheat, no mayo, for lunch. For dinner, roast chicken or broiled fish, steamed carrots, green salad with red bell pepper—always minced by Hannah into perfect tiny squares. No booze, no sugar, no salt, no exceptions. Michael's only vice is—*was*—Coke Zero. He carried a liter bottle with him wherever he went. There was an extra fridge in the garage just to keep those bottles chilled.

And Michael died? Of a *heart attack*?

My phone rings. It's Todd, Hannah's and my editor and Hannah's closest friend, calling from L.A. "Un-fucking-believable," he says.

"I know."

"Here's the plan," Todd says. "I'm driving up to their house—Hannah's house—today. I'll work from there till I can find someone to take the next shift. We can't let her be alone till she's ready to be."

"I'm checking flights," I say.

"Don't. Hannah won't have it. She wants to talk to you every morning when she first wakes up, before she gets out of bed. Can you do that?"

"But I want to be with her now."

"For you?" Todd asks. "Or for Hannah? Because she's clear on what she wants."

Not for nothing is Todd everyone's favorite editor. He wastes no words. "Okay," I say. "I'll stay here. And I'll call her every morning."

"Think about it before you agree. An hour, maybe two on the phone every morning. With a woman whose husband just dropped dead. You worked hard to get that residency. This isn't what your time there is for."

"I don't have to think about it."

"All right," Todd says. "I'll tell her to call you first thing tomorrow morning."

"Or sooner, if she needs to."

"She won't interrupt you. You know how stubborn she is."

"I know how stubborn she *was*," I say, thinking about who I was *before* and who I am now. Hannah will never be the same person who said, "See you tonight, honey," when Michael kissed her good-bye and left for work this morning.

THE NEXT MORNING Hannah calls me at seven her time, ten a.m. mine. I close my laptop and take my phone to the Adirondack chair on my porch and put my feet up on the porch railing.

"I'm listening," I say.

"I can't believe it," she says, her voice thick and low.

"I know, honey."

"I can't believe it," she says again. After a long silence, she says it again. And again.

THE NEXT MORNING Hannah calls me at four a.m. her time.

"You're up early," I say.

"The doc . . . they gave me something to put me to sleep. But it doesn't keep me asleep."

Hannah can't say the word *doctor*. Michael was her doctor. I feel the magnitude of what she's lost beginning to seep into her consciousness.

"I'm lying here looking at my hands," Hannah says. "It's so weird. They look the same as they did yesterday. How can my hands be the same when nothing else is the same?"

My heart hurts. "I know exactly what you mean," I say.

"If I had a cut on my hand, I could look at it every day and see how it was healing," she says. "But I'm looking at my fingers right now and they're all still there and there's no measure of how I'm actually doing."

———————

THE MORNING AFTER that Hannah calls me at noon my time, nine a.m. hers.

"I slept late. I was up till four a.m. I'm so lonely."

"Of course you are."

"Todd's here. We watched TV in bed last night. He read my e-mail for me this morning. It's so good that he's here."

Shouldn't I be there, too? "You know I'll come if you need me," I say.

"I don't. These phone calls, that's what I need from you."

"Todd loves you," I say. "We all love you."

"I hope I'll be able to write again someday."

"You're on heavy meds, honey. When you're feeling a little better and sleeping a little better, you'll go off them and then you'll be able to write again."

"That's not it. Michael was my foundation. He's the reason I could go so far afield in my mind. I was safe to roam around in my imagination all day because I knew when I shut my computer down at dinnertime, Michael would be there, and he'd say, 'Hi, honey,' and then we'd eat the same dinner we always ate and watch the same shows on PBS and go to sleep at our normal time. He was my world. My connection to the real world."

"I get it," I say. "But what you're feeling now—it's going to change."

"How do you know that?"

"Do you remember how I was when you met me?"

Waiting for Hannah's answer, I notice that her breathing is a bit less labored than it was yesterday.

"You were in pieces," she says. "You're better now."

"No one knows that as well as you do."

"You were sleeping on people's couches," Hannah continues. "You've been working hard on yourself, and you're different. More positive. More compassionate. More giving. You have a great life. And you made it all happen. You created a whole new reality for yourself."

"I did," I agree. "With a whole lot of help from my friends. You'll do that, too. It'll just take time."

HANNAH CALLS ME EVERY MORNING when her sleeping pill wears off. I talk to her—listen to her, mostly—for an hour or two, until she says, "I'm going to try to get out of bed now." Then I go back to writing until I meet the swim team for the drive to the pond.

OF COURSE I NEED TO TELL Helena that Michael died. Helena has always liked Hannah, not least because Hannah was such a fan of Helena's and of our relationship.

It's comforting to hear Helena's voice. Compared to the shiny new pennies of my colony friendships, my connection to Helena feels solid, known. Since Hannah has forbidden me to fly across the country for Michael's memorial, Helena promises to go in my place. Hannah reports back that Helena signed my name in the guest book.

"She hardly even knew Michael. She came because she loves you that much," Hannah tells me the next morning.

"Apparently even your husband's death can't stop your campaign to marry me off to Helena," I say, and for the first time since Michael died, Hannah and I laugh together.

"I was so happy before Michael died," she says. "I'm glad I appreciated what I had while I had it. But I don't think I'll ever be happy again."

"It'll be a different kind of happiness. But you'll be happy again," I say. I've spent the past three years saying this to myself without much luck, as Hannah well knows. But we both also know that Hannah is made of stronger stuff, self-esteem-wise, than I am.

"Grief is the biggest part of you right now," I tell her. "But that won't always be true. The rest of your life will get bigger again. You'll grow scar tissue over this wound."

"I'm not sure about that," Hannah says. "I know I'm strong enough to get through this. But is that what the rest of my life is going to be? Getting through the days, instead of being *happy*, the way I used to be?"

"I wonder the same thing," I confess. "It's exhausting, trying to be happy."

"But you're happy now, with your new book and your new friends," Hannah says. I hear the plea in her voice. I understand it. But I'm not going to lie to her.

"Not the way I used to be."

My words ring in our silence. I can't stand doing this to Hannah. But she trusts me to tell her the truth.

"I hate hearing that," Hannah says.

"I know, honey," I say. "I hate that it's true."

—————

LATER THAT DAY I'M WRITING in the colony's air-conditioned library when Otis, a sculptor I've chatted with a few times, comes into the room with a sketchpad in his hand.

"Will it bug you if I sit here and work?" he asks.

"I'd love it if you'd sit there and work," I say. "I'm sick of myself right now."

Otis nods. "All this solitude is awesome when I'm feeling good. It's hell when I'm not."

Our eyes meet and hold. "Right now," Otis says, "not."

"Do you feel like talking about it?" I ask.

"Oh," he says, "I thought everyone knew."

"Maybe everyone else does," I say. "But I don't."

Nine months ago, Otis tells me, he was driving his family minivan through the mountains, taking his wife and daughters to his parents' house for Thanksgiving. As they rounded a blind curve and came up out of a dip, their minivan crashed into a snowplow that had broken down, without lights, in the center of the pitch-black country road. Otis and his wife sustained minor injuries. His thirteen-year-old daughter was permanently paralyzed from the waist down. Their five-year-old daughter died.

"I'm so sorry, Otis," I say, keeping my eyes locked on his, trying not to flinch in the face of his pain.

"Thank you," he says.

The clock on the library wall ticks and tocks.

"Have you been able to work?" I ask him.

"Before the accident, I mostly made big public sculptures. Since the accident, I've been making work about my despair.

Since I got here, I've been making small pieces that deal with my daughter's death more directly."

"That must be so hard."

"It's excruciating," Otis says. "But I think it's helping, too."

"It must be," I say. "Or you wouldn't be doing it."

Otis gazes at me intently. "Voice of experience? Are you writing about hard stuff?"

"Nothing as hard as what you're going through."

"One thing I've learned," Otis says, "is that everyone's hard stuff is hard. Do *you* feel like talking about it?"

I close my laptop, and Otis closes his sketchbook, and for the next couple of hours we talk and laugh and cry a bit together. He asks if I want to see the sculptures he's made since he got here a month ago. We walk across the meadow and down a dirt road to his studio, a huge, white windowed room splattered with gray clay. Otis shows me a dozen or so life-sized ceramic replicas of a little girl's lace-up shoes—some studded with nails, some crushed flat, some topped by a pregnant belly, some flanked by a woman's high heels or by a man's boots.

I look at this man, this new friend, in all his grief and grace. How clearly he knows that the accident that killed his daughter was just that. "I was traveling at the speed limit. I had no time to react," he tells me. "I couldn't afford to blame myself. At that point I was in survival mode, trying to take care of my wife and daughter, staying focused on their needs."

If I'd been behind that wheel, could I have convinced myself, or been convinced, that the crash wasn't my fault? Blaming myself would have made an unthinkable tragedy even worse for everyone involved, including me.

I want to be like Otis. Like Hannah. I want a better relationship with myself. Now, before it's too late.

LOVE IS LOVE IS LOVE, and grief is grief is grief. Otis's pain, Hannah's pain pull me back toward my own. But no matter how low I go, every afternoon, the car ride with the swim team and the baptism in the cold, clear water of the pond take me somewhere lighter and brighter.

Hannah tells me every morning that our conversations are helping her. They're good for me, too. We're so different from each other in so many ways. She hated L.A. and loves Northern California. I was so over NorCal and I love L.A. She's sitting at one end of the mourning train and I'm sitting at the other, but we're riding the same rails.

The distance between where I was three years ago, when Hannah held me together, and where I am now, holding Hannah, gives her a shred of faith, however thin. When she says, "I don't think I'll ever . . . ," when she says she's afraid she'll feel this way for the rest of her life, we both remember the many times I said that to her. Then she says, "I guess there's hope."

"MY THERAPIST TAUGHT ME a trick that kind of works," Hannah tells me one morning. "If I force myself to focus on the present moment, instead of worrying about being alone for the rest of my life, I actually feel a little better."

"That's great."

"I think the Zoloft is kicking in. I'm starting to feel okay on my own."

"Wow, honey. You're amazing," I say. Weeks after her husband's death, Hannah's already more comfortable by herself than I've ever been. It's a flashback to our old dynamic: Hannah walking calmly ahead of me; me trotting distractedly behind her, then running to catch up.

I don't want to be that puppy anymore.

"What's wrong with you today?" Hannah asks.

"I'm fine," I say.

"Please tell me," she says. "I'm so sick of being everyone's *patient*. It would be such a relief to listen to someone else's problems for a change."

"It's my birthday next week. I love being here. But . . . I'm a little lonely."

I wince at my own insensitivity. Hannah just lost her husband of twenty-five years, and *I'm* feeling lonely?

"No biggie," I say. "I'm fine. Tell me how you are."

I feel Hannah wrestling with the transition. In our old relationship, she never would have accepted the shift of attention to her. But now she's working new muscles.

"Twice yesterday I had the experience of *quieting,* just knowing that this is how it is for me now," she says slowly. "I realized it's the desperation of trying to fill the hole that makes me frenetic.

"But the hole can't be filled," Hannah says. "It's going to be there. There's absolutely nothing to do. This is where I am."

I tell Hannah that I did some reading on grief yesterday. "Want me to read you a bit?"

"Please," she says.

"This is from *Daring* by Gail Sheehy," I say. "She was really happy with her husband, and she lost him after twenty-four years, too."

"Her husband was Clay Felker," Hannah says. "He founded *New York* magazine."

"How do you know *everything*?" This is an old joke between us: the Ivy League intellectual who reads Kafka, the high school dropout who reads Kingsolver.

"I tried to think of one good thing about being a widow: more closet space. I knew the worst thing about being a widow: five to seven PM."

"That's my worst time," Hannah says.

"I know," I say.

"So much of grief . . . is raw fear. Would there ever be happy times again? A tearless night? A rising from bed that was not a heroic act? Careless laughter?"

"Spoiler alert," I say. "Gail Sheehy got happy again."

"How long did it take her?" Hannah asks.

This is our deal, mine and Hannah's: we do emphasize the positive, but we do not lie.

"Years," I answer. "But listen to this, from Gail Caldwell's *New Life, No Instructions*.

"We survive grief merely and surely by outlasting it—the ongoing fact of the narrative eclipses the heartbreak within."

"What if I'm too old to outlast my grief?" Hannah says.

I wonder this about myself every single day. It's the geriatric biological clock ticking. "You're not too old for anything," I say, emphasizing the positive while lying just a little bit.

TWENTY

'm aware that for normal mortals, spending a birthday alone is not a thing to dread or fear. Some, including Hannah, who will only name the month, not the date, of her birthday, prefer to "celebrate" that way.

Normal is not a word that anyone would use to describe my relationship to birthdays—others' or my own. At the family gathering where my ex-husband and ex-girlfriend first met the woman who is now my ex-wife, they both wished her luck surviving the month of August for as long as our relationship should live.

Even before I open my eyes, waking up on this birthday feels different. The solitary day I've planned is a long, quiet tunnel, one way in, one way out, no interventions. No one around me knows, so no one will disappoint or rescue me. The day will be as pleasant or unpleasant as I choose to make it.

My phone rings. "I figured out how to be okay," Hannah says without preamble. "It's all about the neural pathways. I can't let the bad thoughts carve grooves in my brain. Only productive thoughts are allowed. If I start thinking about something I have no control over, I let it go and focus on something I can do something about."

"You're so *rational*," I blurt. "I wish I could control myself that way."

"You can."

"How?"

"Don't you have a birthday coming up soon?" Hannah asks.

"It's today, actually."

"Perfect," she says. "Why don't you give yourself a birthday present and spend the day being nice to yourself? Every time you think something bad about yourself, think something good instead."

If this advice were coming from anyone else, I'd dismiss it as feel-good, self-validating Post-its-on-the-bathroom-mirror, Oprah pop psych bullshit. But Hannah doesn't do bullshit.

"If you won't do it for yourself," Hannah says, "do it for the people who love you."

"Huh?"

"If you were okay on your own, you'd stop needing other people to make you feel good about yourself. That's the only bad thing about you. You pull at other people for that."

"That's horrible. God. I'm sorry."

"There's nothing to apologize for. You're human.

"All we can ask of ourselves is that we try to be better," Hannah says. "You're doing that. You're so much smarter emotionally than when you got to L.A. You lost your job and you didn't fall apart. You ended it with Helena, even though you want a partner and you don't know if you'll find someone else. You've helped me so much since Michael died. You've been here with me very single day.

"Everyone else knows these things about you. You just have to work on knowing them about yourself."

I am *not* going to cry, or drown Hannah in the wave of my emotions. "I'll take it under advisement," I say.

"MORNING, SWEETIE," Marta greets me in the dining room. "Coffee?" She waves the pot in my direction.

"Thanks. I'm having tea."

Marta pours herself a mug, adds almond milk, and carries it into the kitchen to order her eggs. I fall into line behind her, greeting the fellow fellows who fall into line behind me.

No one's wishing me a happy birthday.

They don't know it's my birthday. That's the plan, remember?

Whose idea was that? It's a terrible plan.

I scarf down my eggs, wish everyone a productive day, jump on my bike, and pedal toward the dirt path that curves for miles through the woods. The muggy air makes me long for arid L.A. But where will that kind of thinking get me? I'm here now, in a different but equal paradise. I force my focus to the spicy snap of the pine needles shattering beneath my wheels.

My plan is to spend my birthday at the racetrack near the colony, picking daily doubles and communing with my dad. I chain my bike to the fence, pay the entry fee that my dad used to pay for me, and find a spot along the paddock rail, where he and I always hung out before we placed our bets. Despite overwhelming evidence to the contrary, my father remained convinced that watching the jockeys mount the horses allowed him to predict the outcome of each race. "Number seven's nervous," he'd whisper, as if he were sharing insider-trading information. "Look at number five. He's favoring his right front leg."

In honor of my dad and his cockamamie strategies, I bet every race in two-dollar combos that obviate a net win. I toast him with a rubbery racetrack hot dog, raise a plastic cup of warm, foamy racetrack beer. I enlist him to help me pick my losers. He throws in a few words of wisdom, no extra charge.

"Win or lose, just stay in the game," I hear him saying. "Sometimes you might have to give in. But don't ever give up."

I go to the paddock, hang on the rail, watch the jockeys mounting the horses. And then I head to the window to place my next bet.

SINCE THE ER DOC CUT my wedding band off my hand three years ago, I've been wanting a substitute. Every time I glance at my bare ring finger, my stomach sinks, the way it does when I find my credit card missing from its slot in my wallet or my wallet missing from my purse.

This seems a fitting day to shop for a replacement. So after the eighth race, I pedal to the antique store in town. And there, shining inside the dusty display case, I see it. A simple old-gold oval circled by small, sparkling garnets. My ring.

The shopkeeper hands me the tray. I slip the bit of gold onto the ring finger of my left hand. I hold it up, inspect it more closely. The letter *M* is etched into the oval.

"I'll take it," I say.

————

I'D PLANNED TO TAKE MYSELF out to dinner in town, not as a celebration—I've never enjoyed restaurant meals alone—but as a safeguard against blowing my secret. Feeling happy and invincible thanks to my new Wonder Woman ring, I turn my bike toward the colony.

Pedaling up the long, steep driveway, I run into Otis walking back from a hike. I get off my bike and fall into step with him. I ask how he's doing, and we sit on a bench in the garden, falling into another conversation without walls, without niceties, without lies.

I notice the lengthening of the shadows through the pines. "Hey, what time is it?" I ask Otis.

"Whoa! It's dinnertime already. We've been talking for two hours."

I'm amazed. While we were talking, I didn't think once about my birthday or who might have left me a birthday message or anything other than what Otis was saying to me and what I was saying to Otis.

In this I find hope. Maybe what I want—what makes me feel human and engaged and alive and good about myself, or better yet, makes me forget about myself entirely—isn't just other people's attention and approval. What I want is what I have with Otis right now: an exchange of deep thoughts and innermost feelings, held safe in a container of trust. In other words, intimacy.

Wanting an intimate relationship doesn't mean I get one. But to paraphrase Stephen Stills, if I can't be with the one I love, my best insurance policy against a sad, lonely old age is to love the one I'm with. The one who will never leave me, no matter what, for real.

That one, of course, would be me.

Extrovert or not, intimacy junkie or not, I want to be able to have a nice day alone. I want to enjoy my own company, to believe what Hannah keeps telling me, what my dad told me in our final conversation, and God seems to confirm: that I'm good and that I'm loved, every day of the year.

Otis and I walk together to the dining room and join the line for dinner, which happens to be fried chicken, my very favorite colony meal. Simone waves me into the seat she's saved me, and I take my place at the table between her and Donald, a filmmaker who screened his documentary in progress last night. Greta, a German director, asks Donald how he got the permissions for his film. Sarah, a costume designer, compliments its set designs. A composer asks about the score. Full of my day, full of fried chicken, full of myself, I sit back and listen, feeling utterly content.

The dessert bell rings, and then something strange happens. The lights in the dining room go out. Through the darkness Marta emerges from the kitchen, her face lit by the candles on the cake she's carrying. Everyone hoots and hollers as Marta crosses the room and sets the cake in front of me. The lights come back on, and thirty-two people sing "Happy Birthday." To me.

"Make a wish," Riya instructs me.

"How did you guys know—" I sputter.

"Hel-lo," Elaine says. "Facebook much? C'mon—make a wish."

I close my eyes and ask God what to wish for. What I hear is, "You have everything you need."

So the wish I make is "I wish to know that I have everything I need."

As I'm cutting the cake, Otis appears and hands me a small cardboard box. "Open it," he says.

Resting on a bed of shredded newspaper is a tiny sculpture I'd admired in Otis's studio: a six-inch-long, detailed, 1940s pinup-style cheerleader in a pleated miniskirt, leaping skyward, one knee bent, pom-poms waving, her face radiating triumph and joy.

"I love her," I tell Otis.

He smiles. "She reminds me of you."

Phoebe produces a family-sized bottle of Hendrick's. "G and T's, anyone?" she says.

JUST BEFORE MIDNIGHT, full of gin and sloppy gratitude, I tumble into my room. There I find a huge bouquet of white peonies and pinkish-white roses. "The party follows you," the card reads. "Because you are love. And loved. XO, Helena."

I bury my face in the velvety blooms, close my eyes, and breathe in the scent, and the love.

Picking up my phone to call Helena and thank her, I see that I've got new voice mails, e-mails, and texts. Ah, here's my drug. *How do they love me? Let me count the voice mails.*

The phone rings in my hand. It's Hannah. My heart flutters with fear. She never calls me at night.

"Are you okay?" I ask.

"Whew," Hannah says breathlessly. "I almost missed it. I forgot it's three hours later there."

"Almost missed what?"

"Your birthday." She starts to sing "Happy Birthday" comically off-key, then stops halfway through. "Here's your present," she says. "I'm not going to sing to you."

I laugh. "Thanks for that. But you don't care about birthdays. What's gotten into you?"

"I never *used to* care about birthdays," Hannah corrects me. "Who knows what I care about now? You're not the only one who gets to change, you know."

"How could I not know that?" I say. "Look who I've been talking to every morning. I tell you all the time, you're my hero. You amaze me."

Unlike me, Hannah doesn't like what she calls "corny talk," and she'd rather praise than be praised. I wait for her to deflect, deny, minimize my compliment, as she usually does.

"Thank you," Hannah says instead, her voice hoarse with emotion. "That means a lot, coming from you. You're my hero, too."

"Wow, honey," I say. "I'm touched."

"Yeah, well . . . You can tell me about your day tomorrow morning, okay? I mean, it's late there. I mean . . . I gotta go."

Her eagerness to escape the emotions of the moment makes me smile. It occurs to me there was a time, not long ago, when it would have hurt my feelings.

"Good night," I say. "I love you."

"Love you, too," Hannah says, and hangs up.

I tuck myself into bed, stroke the smooth solid gold on the ring finger of my left hand, breathe in the sweet scent of the bouquet.

Best birthday ever, I think. Drifting toward sleep, I wonder what I'll come up with next year. Because it's never too late to try something new.